DATA-FIRST

MARKETING

JANET DRISCOLL MILLER AND JULIA LIM

DATA-FIRST

MARKETING

HOW TO COMPETE AND WIN IN THE AGE OF ANALYTICS

WILEY

Published by John Wiley & Sons, Inc., Hoboken, New Jersey.
Published simultaneously in Canada.

For general information on our other products and services or for technical support, please contact our Customer Care Department within the United States at (800) 762-2974, outside the United States at (317) 572-3993 or fax (317) 572-4002.

Wiley publishes in a variety of print and electronic formats and by print-on-demand. Some material included with standard print versions of this book may not be included in e-books or in print-on-demand. If this book refers to media such as a CD or DVD that is not included in the version you purchased, you may download this material at http://booksupport.wiley.com. For more information about Wiley products, visit www.wiley.com.

Library of Congress Cataloging-in-Publication Data:

Names: Miller, Janet Driscoll, 1971- author. | Lim, Julia, 1968- author.
Title: Data-first marketing : how to compete and win in the age of
    analytics / Janet Driscoll Miller and Julia Lim.
Description: Hoboken, New Jersey : John Wiley & Sons, Inc., [2020] |
    Includes bibliographical references and index.
Identifiers: LCCN 2020022872 (print) | LCCN 2020022873 (ebook) | ISBN
    9781119701217 (cloth) | ISBN 9781119701262 (adobe pdf) | ISBN
    9781119701248 (epub)
Subjects: LCSH: Marketing–Management. | Marketing–Statistical methods.
Classification: LCC HF5415.13 .M5395 2020 (print) | LCC HF5415.13 (ebook)
    | DDC 658.8/3–dc23
LC record available at https://lccn.loc.gov/2020022872
LC ebook record available at https://lccn.loc.gov/2020022873

Cover Design: Wiley
Cover Image: Wiley

Printed in the United States of America

SKY10020253_080320

From Janet:

To my daughters, Emma and Molly: I hope that you will continue always to be strong believers in math and science and let data guide your decisions.

To my parents, Charles and Donna: Thank you for always believing in me and teaching me, from a very young age, that I could be anything and accomplish whatever I put my mind to.

To all of my family and friends: thank you for your continued support during this journey. It has meant the world to me.

From Julia:

To the boy who hid out in the movie theater so he could watch *From Here to Eternity* all day long. You dreamed big and taught me to do the same.

Contents

Foreword

"Where are the hot leads!?" The vice president of sales yelled at me on a regular basis. "These leads stink! Our people can't sell."

I'd respond with something clever like "You've got good leads! Your people just stink at closing!"

In the late 1990s and very early 2000s, I served as the vice president of marketing of several different publicly traded technology companies. The tension at the companies I worked for was common at most organizations and it stemmed from the sales process involving a handoff. Marketing generated the leads and then handed them over to the sales team, who owned them until close.

Back then, I now realize, the marketing and sales departments at the companies I was with weren't aligned because we didn't share common goals based on easy to understand data. Marketing had metrics like how many people subscribed to our email newsletter, how many business cards we collected in the fishbowl at the tradeshow booth, and how many press clips talked about our company. Sales was measured on how much new business they closed and how many existing customers they kept.

Like a marriage on the rocks, we were speaking different languages. We weren't communicating. And it was negatively affecting the business.

In the two decades since my tension-filled encounters with the sales VP, the amount of data available to marketers has exploded. We're able to measure every click in our campaigns and every like in social media. We can see exactly what people do when they visit our site and we can learn much about what's happening in the wider marketplace and with our competitors.

This explosion in the availability of data actually makes that sales-versus-marketing disconnect even worse, because at most companies we're still not aligned. Marketing and sales (and finance too) are still speaking different languages.

The good news is we can do something about the disconnect! Janet Driscoll Miller and Julia Lim are here to show us how in *Data-First Marketing*. This is the book I wish I had back when I was trying to communicate with the sales VP. But more than that, this is the book that would have gotten me speaking the language of the CFO and the CEO and the board of directors.

Data-First Marketing is a deep dive into how to understand modern marketing in our new age of analytics. Janet and Julia show you how to create a process to align your entire organization around business goals so that what we do as marketers is always focused on what's most important for the business.

Understanding data-first marketing means our strategies and tactics, including goals, activities, and campaigns, are clearly defined and measurable within the context of the business as a whole.

I particularly like that the ideas in these pages can be used by large companies like those I used to work for, or for tiny companies of just one person like I run now.

Janet and Julia have been at the forefront of data-driven marketing for many years and write from the perspective of practitioners who have achieved success. They make the ideas both practical and easy to understand.

You will soon read their answer when they ask: "Many of the concepts this book has put forth may seem like common sense. But if the concepts were so simple, why haven't marketers done it?" While you will learn how Janet and Julia answer their own question, I would add another reason: *fear*.

We all face fear in our professional lives. Fear of the strange, of the new, of the untested. It's a natural human response.

It's okay to be fearful of data-first marketing if it is new to you! However, that's not a good reason to ignore the power of what it can do for your company.

We also fear learning a new marketing language. For example, the world of marketing data seems to be filled with an enormous number of three letter acronyms. "CNN and HBR say B2B CMOs need a PIP focused on KPIs around CTR and CPC to drive ROI but need buy-in from the CFO and CEO first." (Do you understand this sentence I just made up?)

To truly achieve marketing success for yourself and your organization, you must overcome your fear of the new. Understanding the data-first marketing approach as outlined in these pages will help eliminate your fear so you can implement the ideas that lead to greatness.

Here's to your success and to your personal fulfillment!

David Meerman Scott
Marketing strategist,
entrepreneur, and best-selling author of eleven books,
including *Fanocracy* and *The New Rules of Marketing & PR*
www.DavidMeermanScott.com
@dmscott

Preface

From Janet

I was first drawn to a career in marketing as a kid. I vividly remember watching the revolutionary Apple Macintosh ad of 1984 during Super Bowl XVIII and the sense of amazement and wonder I felt after watching the ad. It was like nothing I'd seen before in a TV ad. As a young marketer, I was drawn to Apple's "Think Different." campaign, featuring inspirational figures that broke the mold, like Gandhi, Muhammad Ali, John Lennon, and more. I still have a copy of the ad featuring Jim Henson – one of my all-time favorites. I also found myself drawn to the inspirational marketing messages of Nike ads of "Just Do It." or "Stop Dreaming. Start Working." These ads covered my bulletin board. I loved their creativity and the way they inspired me.

While the creativity of marketing drew me to the profession, marketing was beginning to make a profound shift in the early nineties. I entered marketing, in my estimation, at exactly the right time for me. In 1995, barely out of college and working in my first job, I was invited to a nearby business by a friend to be a part of a focus group to evaluate a new tool to find information on the growing Internet. The search engine I was evaluating that night was Yahoo!

In the mid-nineties, as the Internet began exposing a new, graphical format for finding and reading information on the network, I found myself drawn to it. The World Wide Web and its GUI interface offered me a way to marry my creative side with my technical side, so I learned how to program in HTML. The question remained at that time, though: how will this really be adapted for marketing? There weren't many measurement tools in the nineties to understand how marketing efforts on the Internet were affecting a business. Aside from basic traffic information from server logs and tools to process that data like WebTrends, marketers were mostly happy with seeing that people were visiting their websites.

In 1998 GoTo.com, later renamed Overture, launched the first pay-per-click advertising model. The product revolutionized how businesses advertised on the Internet. With this new model, advertisers no longer had to pay solely by impression (the ad being shown). Instead, advertisers could pay for their ads on an action basis – when the searcher clicked on the ad itself and thus visited the advertiser's website. As the pricing model grew in popularity with advertisers and search engines began adding this ad model to their sites, I found myself shifting from a more creative marketer to a more analytical one. Between the website measurement tools being developed, such as Urchin (the precursor to Google Analytics), and new digital advertising options with associated metrics, such as Google AdWords, in a very short time marketers had developed new metrics that better defined marketing key performance indicators than broad measurement tools of the print and TV world, such as BPA audits or Nielsen data respectively. These metrics were *exact*.

I found myself shifting too. After being laid off once and surviving a layoff at my next company, I longed for a way to prove my worth to the business I worked for. Digital marketing gave me the best chance at exactly measuring my impact, and the impact of all of our team's marketing efforts, on the business. I began to embrace data and statistics, and I found ways to use them to bolster my position. While I began my career in marketing fully expecting to harness my artistic creativity, I find that I now channel my analytical side so much more.

In 2005 I founded my own search marketing agency, Search Mojo (now renamed Marketing Mojo), focused on search engine optimization (SEO) and paid search advertising. One question I ask all account manager candidates interviewing with our firm is, "Do you see yourself as a more creative person or a more analytical person?" There's no right or wrong answer to this question, per se, but I expect that many recent college graduates entered the marketing field for similar reasons that I did. They saw enormously creative business-to-consumer ads that inspired them. And while there is some artistic creativity in search advertising, analytics play a much larger role today. If you don't enjoy spreadsheets and math, you may not enjoy what marketing has become.

There is, however, still a long way to go. Today, we have more data and tools available to us as marketers than ever before. As an agency owner over the past fourteen years, I've seen so many clients, large and small, with poor measurement implementation or the inability to connect the data points to provide them with a full understanding of their results. Just last year a client with over 1,500 employees confessed that they were storing their incoming website leads in a spreadsheet, then entering each lead by hand into the sales CRM. Yikes.

Today the wealth of information available to us as marketers can seem overwhelming. I encourage you instead to think of the data available as an opportunity. I wrote this book with Julia to help clarify where disconnects exist between the marketing team and the rest of the company and to help close that gap. I wrote it so that other marketers can see the value that marketing data brings to strengthening your positions and reinforcing the marketing team's value to the organization. I've added many actual examples to illustrate mistakes as well as fantastic successes when *the right data* is implemented and utilized correctly in an organization. I hope we can help you create a dynamic shift in your company and solidify the value that your marketing team brings to your organization.

From Julia

Armed with my very new MBA, I joined a web hosting company (originally part of AOL) that would later be merged into UUNET in the late nineties. What a fantastic time to be a marketer in technology! We were truly pioneers; everything we did was the first or one of the first of its kind. We were the first to launch co-location services. We were the one of the first companies to launch hosted ad servers and ecommerce platforms. We dominated the Lotus Notes hosting market. We coined the term "enterprise hosting." Everything we did was new; we defined this very large and rapidly growing market and set its direction. How would I ever top that experience?

A few years after the dot.com bust, I joined a network monitoring startup. I was employee number five, and the first dedicated marketing resource. Despite the extreme lack of sleep, I loved the experience. This was another "greenfield" opportunity; not the market itself this time – network monitoring had been around for a while with huge incumbents like IBM and HP – but the opportunity to create marketing strategy, programs, and processes, really everything, from scratch. The truly fortuitous part of this is that this is exactly when digital marketing was beginning to revolutionize not only how we could reach our customers online, but also how much we could actually do and how quickly. I didn't have bureaucracy to cut through or a "this is how we've always done it" attitude/culture to get around. I evaluated digital marketing tools and services purely on their own merit. Is this the best way to generate qualified leads for sales? Is this the best bang for my marketing buck? ROI wasn't a "pie-in-the-sky" idea; it was vital for a boot-strapped startup like us. If a tool, program, or campaign didn't produce or perform an absolutely necessary function, we didn't do it again. We didn't have the time or the money to waste.

I continued my education on the job. Digital marketing appealed to the nerd in me. I was our Salesforce.com administrator and defined every field. We were an early adopter of marketing automation; I defined every one of those fields as well, plus the integration with Salesforce.com. I met Janet, who was just starting her own SEO agency (later helping us with digital advertising too). During our engagement, she was my partner in really exploring what the new digital marketing tools could do. Because I defined all the data fields plus the sales and marketing processes to ensure data governance, we were able to pull ROI reports out of our new systems and make smarter decisions about what programs, campaigns, and content we should produce to achieve our goals.

Since that initial experience of setting up ROI reporting capabilities across multiple digital marketing platforms in a greenfield environment, I went to two other companies that had existing databases and sales processes, and while I spent more time on evaluating and cleaning up data (a *lot* of time on cleaning up data), the fundamentals were the same. Set up your marketing/sales databases and the processes that would feed those databases from real marketing campaigns so that I could actually pull reports that showed marketing value.

I listed a lot of what happened in detail because I've come to understand that most marketers do not get these kinds of opportunities or learning experiences. With this experience and background, I started to assume that everyone thinks this way: *Data is my friend. I'm going to collect as much data as possible because I'm not sure exactly how I'll use it later or need to filter it but I'd rather have the data than not be able to do the analysis. In the end, everything I do needs to be able to be tied to actual sales for the company.* My epiphany happened in week one after joining Janet's agency.

Janet reached out to me when I was between jobs and looking for my next adventure. I hadn't worked for an agency before, and I admired Janet, her brain, and her commitment to getting things right. (I'd already had my rude awakening about bureaucracy and how it kills initiative and what I had naively thought was everyone's desire to get the job done "right.") As a former customer of Marketing Mojo (twice), I was a good resource for training the rest of the team on what a customer expects from their SEO and digital advertising engagements – or so I thought.

In the training, I focused on "conversion." I had noticed that the "conversion" in the SEO reports, for example, was not necessarily what I thought of as a conversion from a business marketing sense. The SEO reports were pulling from Google Analytics and tied to defined goals in that platform. I tried to explain that to a B2B marketer in particular, "conversion" ideally isn't just a click-through or a website visit; it needs to be tied to pipeline or revenue. I then took them through an example of what I meant, showing a data flow from website (e.g., intake form) to a marketing automation platform (which housed marketing-defined data including lead activities) to a CRM like Salesforce.com (which housed actual opportunities, pipeline, and revenue tied to the leads that came in through the form, got processed in the marketing automation stage, and eventually and hopefully were qualified enough to pass for direct sales interaction). This, I thought, is how marketers think about conversion and would want to measure it.

Crickets.

Well, maybe not that bad, but it wasn't too far off. I was then told an astonishing thing, which interaction with multiple prospects and customers across a variety of industries over the last two years has only confirmed. Our customers aren't doing this. And there was also maybe the tongue-in-cheek comment that they didn't go to Harvard and MIT.

My turn for crickets. What do you mean everyone else doesn't do this? At least to the extent of understanding that marketing conversions must be tied to pipeline and revenue, right?

So, just in case, I'm here to tell you that you definitely don't have to have gone to Harvard and MIT to able to work with data like this and actually use it to measure ROI and make smarter decisions in marketing. This reminds me a little of that part in *Moneyball,* where the stats people are called propeller-heads or something derisive like that. That's okay; I can own being a nerd.

But what I couldn't seem to get past was the idea that other marketers didn't think this way. Was it true? How could it be true? Given the possibilities with data that digital marketing served up, this was absolutely the direction everyone should at least be heading toward, wasn't it?

That smack in the face of my belief that everyone does some version of this was a wake-up call, and I started to pay more attention. Why weren't people doing this? What were the real reasons behind it? And how could I help?

When Janet and I were working through different ideas for this book, we kept dancing around topics having to do with data, analytics, and ROI. (One potential topic I did way too much research on was tying quantum theory to digital marketing – yes, yes, I know, but really it was fascinating and oddly amusing.)

Between the time we started writing and the time we finished the manuscript, there have been two multibillion-dollar acquisitions in this space. This just confirms for us that this is the right topic at the right time. Like the advent of digital marketing before it, marketing data analytics will be a sea change for the field of marketing, and we hope that this book helps you navigate it.

Introduction

UNCERTAINTY ABOUT THE CMO ROLE AS MARKETING IS ASKED TO TAKE ON MORE

The chief marketing officer (CMO) is under attack. In 2019, Forrester predicted the decline of CMO titles stating that "2020 marks the beginning of a final, desperate fight for CMO relevance" (Johnston, 2019).

For a while now, it's been widely known that the CMO has the shortest tenure of any executive in the C-suite (Korn Ferry, 2020). On top of that, in the last couple of years, there have been some very high-profile examples of big business-to-consumer (B2C) companies, like Walmart, Johnson & Johnson, and McDonalds, that have eliminated the position entirely and instead have installed people in less broad roles, such as chief growth officer, chief marketing technology officer, and chief customer experience officer. So what has changed? As it turns out – almost everything.

The new digital economy has disrupted traditional business models – from transportation and supply chain to music and publishing and beyond – leaving businesses scrambling to keep up, innovate, or be left behind. It has spawned completely new industries and fundamentally changed how we research, buy, review, and communicate with one another. In a few short decades, the digital economy has come to dominate even how we live our lives. It has changed buyers; consumers are much more tech savvy, and they have expectations – convenience, ease of purchase, and personalization – set by companies like Amazon, which spends billions in R&D every year.

The average buyer intrinsically knows what is possible when it comes to digital marketing today – from targeted ads and remarketing (e.g., those ads that show up on YouTube for the product you were

1

just looking at) to new video and social media channels. If the average consumer is now tech savvy, CEOs and other business executives are even more so. More informed CEOs, CFOs, and COOs demand more from the CMO as the leadership of marketing teams that are being asked to compete in completely new channels, sometimes even required to create those channels as a source of growth and innovation for their companies.

In May 2017, Coca-Cola appointed James Quincey as the new CEO. As part of the changes he brought, the role of global CMO disappeared and marketing, customer, and commercial leadership strategy were combined into one function under Francisco Crespo, who became the new chief growth officer, reporting to the CEO. At the same time that the CMO role disappeared, a new Chief Innovation Officer was appointed and the CIO started reporting directly to the CEO "to increase visibility and focus on efforts to digitize all aspects of the company's business" (Schultz, 2017).

Two years after it eliminated the role of CMO to create an expanded chief growth officer role, Coca-Cola brought the CMO position back, but with new expectations, as illustrated in this quote from Coca-Cola CEO James Quincey:

> There's a much greater intersection and integration of how to engage with consumers and shoppers. . . . And therefore, bringing together in one group the classical marketing pieces with a customer piece with a commercial piece and with the strategy, underpinned with the digital engagement, is what's going to allow us to more seamlessly operate in this new environment. (Ives, 2019)

At heart, the uncertainty surrounding the role of the CMO today is a reflection of the difference between what marketing is and what business leaders think marketing could and should be. There is tremendous pressure on marketing leadership to lead the charge for their companies when it comes to competing and winning in the digital marketplace, and any failures in the short term, fairly or unfairly, are often laid at their feet. Marketing leadership is expected to navigate rapidly changing consumer expectations, identify new digital opportunities, and master any and every new digital technology that can help along the way. Just keeping on top of the new technologies is a constant battle as marketing technology (martech) continues to explode – add in everything else on top of that, and the role of the CMO just got exponentially tougher.

REINVENTING MARKETING STARTS WITH DATA AND ANALYTICS

CMOs and the marketing function must reinvent themselves. If they fail to do so themselves, it will be done for them – when it's out of their control and probably not to their benefit. This is a massive opportunity for the ones who get it right, and it starts with data and analytics.

Marketing leaders who think that the field is the same and that digital marketing is just a new set of tools and channels to explore will lose out to those who understand that there has been a fundamental change to marketing that must reverberate through the people, processes, and technology that make up how marketing is accomplished in each company.

Thanks to the digital economy and the ever growing martech that we use to exploit it, there is now a fourth critical dimension to marketing – data, or more specifically, the ability to use analytics to glean meaningful information from the vast amount of data available to all modern marketers (See Figure I.1). Data is the new marketing battlefield – from the information that potential buyers provide about themselves on social media or on your digital properties to the quantitative results you have on your sales and marketing operations. In the Age of Analytics, it is this data – captured, filtered, and interpreted intelligently using the lens of your unique business goals – that can create competitive advantages for any business and showcase the true value of what marketing can and should be.

Using data and analytics for competitive advantage is not a new idea, and not just for marketing. But saying something and doing it can

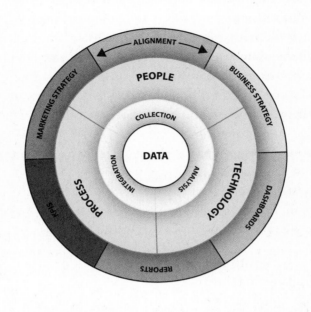

FIGURE I.1   Data-First Marketing Framework

be worlds apart. Data-driven marketing is a term that has been used increasingly over the past few years, but as practiced today, it doesn't go far enough to truly transform marketers and the organization to get the most out of the ever-increasing mountain of data available to all of us today. And that is where data-first marketing comes in.

DATA-FIRST MARKETING PROVES MARKETING'S VALUE

Data-first marketing is a new marketing strategy that focuses on intelligently utilizing the vast amount of marketing data available today in order to create true competitive advantage in any industry. It combines data-driven marketing with business strategy and goals and requires a top-down transformation of people, processes, technology, data, and culture.

The marketing leaders who win will embrace data and move rapidly to take advantage of being first adopters in their respective industries. With marketing data analytics, these marketing leaders can clearly show the rest of the business just how important marketing is to overall business success with metrics that prove it.

Not everyone will do this, and truthfully not everyone can do it, as we see every day in our own practice. The old adage holds true: if it were easy, everyone would do it. A recent Forbes Insight survey conducted for Treasure Data, "Data versus Goliath: Customer Data Strategies to Disrupt the Disrupter," asked 400 executives (CMOs, heads of marketing, chief data or analytics officers, and heads of customer experience) at $1billion-plus companies how far along they were when it came to data-driven marketing. Some of the highlights:

- Only 1 in 4 executives report they are able to fully leverage data that is available to them.
- Only 13% consider they've taken the necessary steps to ensure they're making the most of customer data.
- 65% say customer data analytics has not yet enhanced their competitive capabilities while only 1% report a significant shift.
- In two years, they expect this to change dramatically – 40% anticipate a significant shift in their competitive capabilities from mastering their data.

The opportunity is right in front of us, right now. It's not just the CMO that is in danger of becoming obsolete. Competing and winning in the Age of Analytics requires each marketer, from CMO to staffer, to embrace data-driven marketing. Our data-first marketing strategy, along with the five steps we've detailed in this book, are meant to help you get there.

We have broken this book up into two parts:

- Part I is geared to marketers and C-suite executives, providing an overview of data-first marketing principles and their value to businesses, from large to small. Small to mid-size enterprises, in particular, may find it not only easier to adopt data-first marketing but also to use it to "level the playing field" if they are competing with much larger businesses with deeper pockets. If "everyone knows" they should be doing this, why aren't they already doing it? We explore the challenges and the obstacles along the way to data-first marketing adoption and provide tips to overcome them.

- Part II is designed mostly for marketers and focuses on a blueprint with the five steps we've defined for marketing organizations to begin their data-first transformation. We have included a self-assessment to help you locate where your organization currently sits on the Data-First Marketing Maturity Model; this can be completed by anyone in the organization. Step 1 describes the marketing-to-business alignment that is fundamental for everything else that comes after. Step 2 dives into data, from strategy to integration to governance. Step 3 provides practical tips for marketers to analyze their own data. We're not data analysts, and for the kinds of analysis we include here, we don't have to be to start delivering insights. Step 4 starts to apply data-first marketing to daily activities, providing a Data-First Marketing Campaign Framework and examples of how and why data helps us define and execute what it is we do faster, smarter, and more efficiently. And finally, Step 5 delves into developing and hiring the right skillsets for our staff and beginning to build a true data-first marketing culture, where data is the first thing you think of and not the last or after the fact.

We wrote this book to help marketers, just like us and just like our clients, as we all must make this transformation to embedding data and analytics in our daily work lives. Like all major change, it's not comfortable and it's certainly not easy, but it will be absolutely worthwhile the next time your CEO asks about a campaign and in addition to showing a picture of the creative, you can show a chart that shows new leads, new pipeline, or new revenue that can be tracked back to that campaign.

PART

I

Data-Driven Marketing Is Not Enough

CHAPTER 1

Marketing in the Age of Analytics

PROVING MARKETING'S VALUE TO THE BUSINESS

In 2006, I (co-author Julia) met the CMO of a VoIP startup at a local technology marketing event. Founded in 2004, it was well-funded to the tune of $80 million after a couple of rounds of investment. This was clearly a competitive space, with other VoIP startups investing heavily in marketing and advertising to establish themselves, in addition to the very large and well-known phone company competitors who already "owned" the customers that the upstarts were trying to steal. The main business strategy seemed to be to acquire as many new customers as quickly as possible, but customer acquisition costs were high while revenue per customer was not, as VoIP's main competitive edge was being the low-cost alternative to traditional phone call plans, in particular for international calls.

In a discussion with the CMO, she talked about the search engine optimization (SEO) that her team was doing – optimizing for something like 15,000 keywords. To say I was speechless was probably an understatement. I had several thoughts (none of which I actually blurted out, thank goodness). *Fifteen thousand keywords? How was that even possible? Were there really fifteen thousand keywords around VoIP? How many people did she have on her team, whether in-house or at an agency?* This was years before Amazon came to be so dominant; with all the brands that they sell, if Amazon said they were optimizing their website for fifteen thousand keywords, I would believe them and maybe consider that number on the low side since they offer millions of products. But all this startup had was VoIP services.

Let's look at this another way. Let's say that her SEO team spent 10 hours optimizing the website for each keyword, at 10,400 work hours per person in a year, that would require dedicating nearly 15 people just to do this one task, and that doesn't include the keywords research, content development, monitoring and reporting, analysis, technical SEO tasks, and more that are all required for SEO. How could her team effectively optimize for that many keywords? The answer really is that they could not, and within the year, I was not surprised to hear that that well-funded startup shut its doors.

Volume Metrics versus Value Metrics

Beyond the disbelief in optimizing for that number of keywords (or questioning if that was even a good idea) was the realization that there is something very fundamentally different regarding how marketers look at the metrics that make up what it is that we do.

> One of the data challenges many marketers must overcome is a bias for volume metrics over value metrics. Volume metrics track performance or efficiency. Value metrics, in contrast, assess the quality of an interaction or its impact on the customer relationship and on profitability. (Starita, 2019)

Marketers are seduced by volume metrics. Why wouldn't we be? They make us look good. *Website traffic is up 100% year over year. We had 2 million visits to our website last month*. With numbers like those, the outcome could only be good for the business, right?

But if you look more closely, you can see that volume metrics like these are only the beginning of the story. It's value metrics that can tell you more about why these numbers are important for the business. *Why is traffic up so much? Is it due to specific content on the site? Is traffic up on the products and services pages or is it up on job listings? And most importantly, can I connect these traffic increases to actual pipeline or revenue for the business?*

Volume metrics like website traffic are easy to get; they are the first things you see in most out-of-the-box performance reports. By contrast, value metrics require some digging, and the knowledge behind what you are doing to make sure you are digging in the right directions. Even trickier is trying to tie any kind of metric to revenue. This usually requires some level of data integration since numbers like website traffic can sit in a completely different database or platform from sales numbers, not to mention requiring some level of coding or workflow automation to track a lead from a website visit, through all the other marketing interactions they might have along the buyer's journey all the way to a possible sale. It should not be any surprise that the more "valuable" the value metric, the harder it seems to be able to achieve.

Back to the VoIP startup example. Perhaps the thinking went like this:

CMO to the CEO: *We are optimizing the website for 15,000 keywords.*

Translation: *Look how much work we are doing! Look at all the work you can tell the VCs that they are getting for that big investment they made in the company. What we do is important and complex – just look at how many keywords we actively optimize to make sure we show up on page one of Google searches for every long-tail term.*

Perhaps focusing on SEO and likely digital ads was the marketing strategy for rapid customer acquisition at volume. But if I were the CEO, that's not the first number I would want; the first would be *how many new customers did SEO bring in?*

It's very shortsighted to think that you can trot out volume metrics to show how well you are doing – in a board meeting, in a monthly agency or client meeting, or the like – and not be asked why. More and more, marketers are being asked to prove it – by CEOs, CFOs, sales, clients – and that brings up a whole new set of challenges that many marketers are failing to overcome.

We live in the Age of Analytics surrounded by data, but that doesn't mean that we have the right mindset, skills, and experience to use it in our daily marketing tasks to do more, faster, better. We know we should be pushing toward a data-driven marketing model, but what does that really mean for our marketing teams, and how can we get there? In this book, we try to answer these questions and define a data-first marketing strategy that is achievable by everyone, from large company to single-person business, and that, first and foremost, ensures you never have to settle for volume metrics to show marketing's value to the business.

DIGITAL TRANSFORMATION LEADS TO THE AGE OF ANALYTICS

Who could have known just how much our world would change in a few short decades because of technology? Since the invention of the World Wide Web in 1989, we have experienced a dot.com boom and bust, the rise and dominance of mobile, Internet video, and social media platforms that consume people's time and attention, the emergence of cloud computing and big data along with the tools needed to make them ubiquitous and meaningful, and much more.

The digital marketing transformation we focus on in this book that spawned actionable data and a whole new slew of marketing technologies started a little over a decade ago. But the roots of digital marketing can be traced to about 10–12 years before that – with the next 10 years spent shaking out which technologies would survive.

When we took a look back at the major milestones for digital marketing, we realized that we could divide the digital marketing revolution so far into three "ages" – the Age of Discovery, the Age of Reckoning and finally, where we are now, the Age of Analytics (see Figure 1.1). From the figure, you can see that when a new age starts, the previous age may still continue for a time. For example, the Age of Discovery is characterized by foundational digital marketing

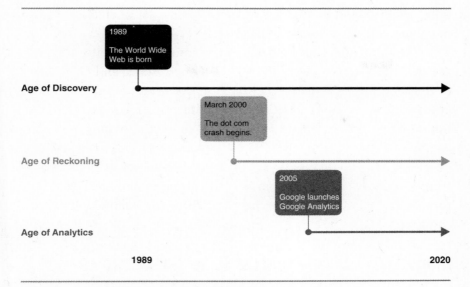

FIGURE 1.1   Ages of Digital Marketing.

(Thank you to Scott Brinker of chiefmartec.com and HubSpot for kindly letting us borrow the term "Age of Reckoning," which we use a bit differently but first saw in his 2nd Golden Age of Martech graphic.)

technologies such as the World Wide Web in 1989, but new foundational technologies are continually emerging, such as data-driven TV ad targeting, which offers the type of audience targeting previously only found in digital advertising, instead of the traditional and imprecise age and gender segmentation that is all TV was able to offer.

The Age of Discovery

The Age of Discovery (see Figure 1.2) began in 1989 with the birth of the World Wide Web, making websites as we know them today possible; the first commercial website with ads, Global Network Navigator, was created in 1993. It was in this period that the foundational and pioneering technologies for what we do in digital marketing today were launched.

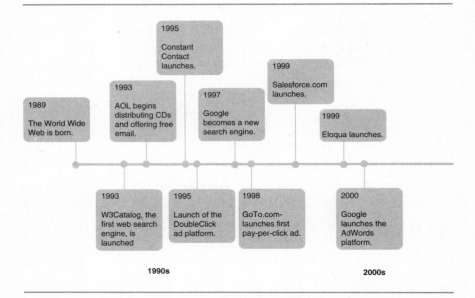

FIGURE 1.2 Age of Discovery: Foundational Digital Marketing Technologies.

(Please note: We clearly could not include every company and every milestone in the timeline so we tried to show the most readily recognizable and/or "firsts.")

In 1996, there were only 100,000 websites, compared to over 1 billion websites today. The most popular sites were early search engines and online communities like AOL and CompuServe, where people just went to check their email or chat with other subscribers. For the most part, commercial websites were online billboards and measurement still followed traditional advertising methods using "eyeballs" or impressions.

By the end of the first part of the Age of Discovery, AOL had grown to more than 23 million subscribers and along with the first blast email programs came spammers. Google launched their ubiquitous search engine. Both Eloqua (an early leader in the marketing automation space, now folded into the Oracle Marketing Cloud) and Salesforce (not the first sales CRM but certainly the 800-pound gorilla for B2B companies) also launched, pushing digital marketers to begin to understand databases and capabilities that went far beyond keeping customer contact information in Excel spreadsheets. And Google launched their highly successful AdWords platform, building on the pay-per-click model introduced by GoTo.com.

Digital Marketing Enables Precise Measurement

Digital advertising is a great example of the true difference between then and now, and traditional and digital when it comes to tracking and measurement. Measuring the effectiveness of print advertising has always been vague and imprecise. Advertising in newspapers and periodicals has been around since the 1800s with advertisers doing their best to match their ads to publications with audiences they were trying to reach. Print ad costs were tied to circulation numbers, first provided by the publication itself (and often padded) and eventually at least audited by a third-party to verify a publication's potential audience for ads. The key word here is "potential" because without user-action-based measurement, you have no idea how many people actually see your ad. Let's be real: people don't buy magazines to read the ads. When you buy a print ad, you are buying access to the publication's subscriber base; you are buying and can only measure "potential" eyeballs or impressions and not actual interaction with the ad. There are some tactics you can use to try to measure engagement better – special offer codes, vanity URL's, dedicated phone lines, and so on – but you will never be able to capture the actual number of "eyeballs."

By contrast, digital ads are measured more tangibly using pay-per-click calculations. Given the choice, why would you ever pay for "potential" eyeballs when instead you can pay for only the people who actually click on your ad? Like many digital marketing innovations, pay-per-click opened up a different level of accuracy when it comes to ROI reporting. Digital ad platforms include extensive tools and reporting for engagement; they can measure *every time* a lead clicks on the call-to-action built into your ad, leading the visitor to your website, preferably a custom landing page where you can ask for additional information such as name, email, company, title, and the like. The more relevant your content, the better chance you have of your visitors identifying themselves.

This is important for two reasons. First, you have now engaged a potential buyer directly and can contact them and nurture them along their buyer's journey. Second, if you have technology like cookies and marketing automation in place, you can match this specific visitor with their past actions, which were still being tracked and recorded even before you knew the specifics of who they are. Tying this information all together gives a full picture of every time and every way marketing touched that lead – critical data when it comes time to analyze marketing campaign performance and effectiveness that leads to actual pipeline and revenue for a company.

This capability to track the buyer's journey across multiple channels required a level of maturity and integration of the digital marketing platforms that survived into the Age of Reckoning (see Figure 1.3).

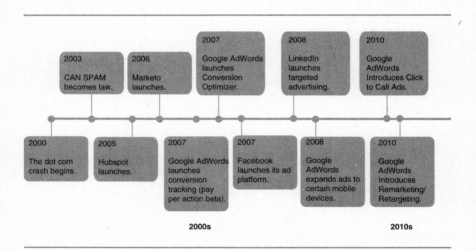

FIGURE 1.3   Age of Reckoning: Dot.com Bust and Surviving Martech.

The Age of Reckoning

The dot.com bubble in the latter half of the 1990s was a time of tremendous growth for tech companies. "Startup" became a household word. It seemed like everyone and their brother had a great idea for a new tech company, in the hopes of having it take off and being able to reap the great monetary rewards, and the more the market grew, the bigger the hype and momentum.

> The value of the NASDAQ, home to many of the biggest tech stocks, grew from around 1,000 points in 1995 to more than 5,000 in 2000. Companies were going to market with IPOs and fetching huge prices, with stocks sometimes doubling on the first day. It was a seeming wonderland where anyone with an idea could start making money. (Geier, 2015)

In 2000, the bubble burst. No matter how great the idea was or how addictive the branding (pets.com sock puppets, anyone?), if a business couldn't actually figure out a way to make money, it could not survive. Technology in particular required a "killer app" to really take off: an application that had potentially widespread adoption that could be monetized.

Digital marketing was similarly affected; early-stage digital advertising, ecommerce platforms and more either died out or were purchased and repurposed. Any new martech emerged with their eyes on the prize – practical applications that could be monetized. Most of the mainstays of today's digital marketing were launched in this period, including Google AdWords (2000, also in the Age of Discovery), Facebook Ads (2007), LinkedIn Ads (2005), and YouTube ads (2005).

Alongside digital advertising came marketing automation platforms like Eloqua (1999, also in the Age of Discovery), Marketo (2008), and HubSpot (2005) that make it possible for a single marketer to pull in thousands, even millions, of prospects and automate the qualification process that whittles them down to only those who are real sales leads. Outreach in the digital age is completely different for more companies than ever before – and not just for the Fortune 500 companies that have ad budgets and ad agencies that can reach millions via traditional advertising. Salesforce.com (as mentioned previously in the Age of Discovery) launched the first iteration of its customer relation management (CRM) platform in 1999; it wasn't the first CRM, but it was the one to revolutionize the industry and today dominates the market with around 20% of the global CRM market, according to research firm Gartner.

As described in the traditional/digital advertising comparison above, the broad availability and adoption of martech tools means any company can track every single click when someone engages with your online ad. Plus, marketers create "carrots" along a buyer's journey – such as special offers or relevant content – to entice buyers to give you more information about themselves, which in turn enables increasingly personalized outreach and tracking, both automated from marketing and in-person with a salesperson after they've been qualified as a real sales lead. Multiply this information by thousands or millions and you can see how quickly customer data can grow.

For B2C companies, this explosion of data from our new martech tools and platforms can approach the size of big data, requiring specialized analysis using advanced data analytics tools that can handle the volume, expert data scientists and analysts, and even artificial intelligence and machine learning tools to achieve predictive analytics.

For the rest of us, and in particular for B2B companies, the vast amount of marketing data readily available poses a huge opportunity, but most marketers are ill-equipped to take advantage because they lack both the skillset and the data-first mentality we explore in this book. One could point to the lack of practical education on marketing data analytics, but as we have shown, the technology moves so quickly, it has been difficult for anyone to keep up.

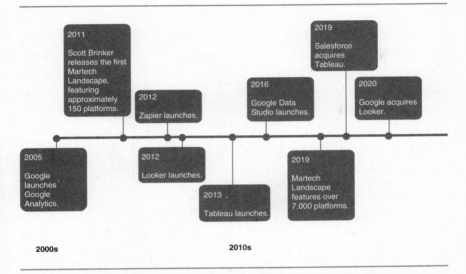

FIGURE 1.4   Age of Analytics: Gleaning Insight from the Explosion of Customer Data.

For all marketers, the explosion of marketing data heralded the Age of Analytics (see Figure 1.4), when they need to have the tools and know-how to transform data into actionable and positive results for the business.

The Age of Analytics

The Age of Analytics is characterized by the explosive growth of marketing data and the necessary data access/management, visualization, and analytics tools that are emerging to help marketers deal with increasing data overload. Google Analytics was launched in 2005 after Google acquired Urchin Software, marking the beginning of our Age of Analytics timeline. For many marketers, it was their first experience with analytics and because of that is very influential in defining what marketers expect from any analytics tools coming after it.

As it evolves, digital marketing continues to generate new channels like social media platforms, new technologies like mobile,

FIGURE 1.5   2011 Martech Vendor Landscape.
Source: Courtesy of Scott Brinker, chiefmartec.com.

connected devices and the Internet of Things, new martech like video conferencing and web streaming – all of which come with their own set of data. IBM Marketing Cloud's "10 Key Marketing Trends for 2017" estimated that 90% of the data in the world today has been created in the last two years alone, and it just keeps growing.

Looking at just the martech portion of this data equation is daunting. In 2011, chiefmartec.com created a martech landscape of about 100 vendors (see Figure 1.5.)

By 2019, this martech landscape ballooned to over 7,000 vendors under dozens of separate categories, comprising a market size of $121.5 billion worldwide, almost double the 2018 valuation (see Figure 1.6).

In addition to the complexity of mastering what seems like an ever-growing list of digital marketing technologies is the need to

FIGURE 1.6   2019 Martech Vendor Landscape.

Source: Courtesy of Scott Brinker, chiefmartec.com.

access, manage, integrate, and analyze each tool's specific set of data. Underlying all of these martech tools and platforms is data, whether it is an actual database, in the case of marketing automation and CRMs, or it is the metrics about performance, reach, and so on that are generated by the use of each martech tool.

Social media also offers valuable data, provided by people themselves, that the platforms make available to advertisers for targeting; obviously recent privacy concerns and scandals have had an impact on how and how much of this data is available, but it has not slowed down advertising revenue. In 2004, social media was defined by MySpace with about 1 million users. In 2019, Facebook alone had 2.3 billion users, and an estimated 1 out of 3 people use social media globally and 2 out of 3 online users do so. The amount of data available from social media is staggering – from demographics (e.g., title, company, and gender) to likes and dislikes and the groups that people join.

But data is nothing without the ability to interpret it and utilize it to make smarter, faster decisions. More specifically, we are talking about marketing data analytics that sifts through customer data and relevant sales and operational data (internal and external) in order to define personalization, engage customers, improve segmentation and targeting, and develop more effective and targeted content and campaigns.

Data analytics is the next big thing in digital marketing. Two major acquisitions in digital marketing last year involved large martech players snatching up data visualization and analytics companies, buying their way into adding this functionality to their own platforms quickly. In 2020, Google purchased Looker for $2.6 billion. In 2019, Salesforce purchased Tableau for a whopping $15.7 billion. Salesforce CEO Marc Benioff described the strategic positioning in the acquisition press release: "We are bringing together the world's #1 CRM with the #1 analytics platform. Tableau helps people see and understand data, and Salesforce helps people engage and understand customers. It's truly the best of both worlds for our customers – bringing together two critical platforms that every customer needs to understand their world."

Just to emphasize, Tableau is worth $15.7 billion to Salesforce, more than 10 times Tableau's annual revenue. Clearly Salesforce is placing a big bet that their target customers (B2B companies) recognize the need for data analytics and will pay for it.

B2B companies, in particular, have the opportunity today to be among the first companies to take advantage of data and analytics in their respective industries and create true competitive advantage. The challenge, however, is that for companies to succeed, they must go far beyond most of the data-driven marketing that we see today and that everyone else also does – such as using Google Analytics and looking at metrics in isolated martech platforms – and instead embrace a true organizational transformation to get to the next level of data-driven marketing.

BUILDING A MARTECH STACK MULTIPLIES THE DATA AND NEED FOR ANALYTICS

Starting in 2004, I (co-author Julia) remember the process of adding digital marketing channels and tools as the industry began to shake out in the Age of Reckoning and standardize on certain key martech platforms that had proven their value. First, of course, was the website, then the blog, with SEO and Google Analytics for rudimentary traffic analysis, which gave us our initial digital marketing performance reports. Then came Salesforce, customized for both marketing and sales, which provided email lists for blast communications in Constant Contact. Salesforce was a revelation because it gave me my first take at real ROI and customer data reports using the deceptively simple yet powerful Salesforce reporting engine, which let us easily slice and dice and filter using any data fields that we could capture. If I wanted to be able to run a report that showed the lead source of all closed-won opportunities for new customers only, I had to check if fields existed for this information and create any fields I needed, then make sure they were actually populated with data, then run the report. Constant Contact, my email marketing platform, also had performance reports on each email campaign that I sent out. Then came digital advertising, first on Google AdWords and then on LinkedIn – all of which had their own set of performance reports.

Every time I added a tool to my martech stack, it multiplied the amount of data I needed to analyze the performance and efficiency of my marketing campaigns. By the time I added the Eloqua marketing automation platform, I was more than ready to start integrating all of these different marketing data sources in order to standardize on a combination of Eloqua and Salesforce for comprehensive, multichannel and multi-attribution reporting for all of my marketing campaigns. Just as Salesforce was the sales CRM, Eloqua became my marketing CRM, enabling me to capture and manage more customer data than I had ever had access to before, both because of increased lead volume and the increased amount of information per lead, from demographics to user actions like registering for a webinar, clicking on an email link, or downloading a white paper, that were automatically registered and saved in the database, tied to that specific lead. Eloqua allowed me to automate the capture of this data, any follow-up via email communications or alerts, and the consolidation of all of this data in one easily accessible database.

Every step of adding to the digital martech stack also added analytics capabilities, even if it was just from basic performance reports. But the complexity and size of our growing digital marketing stack and data stores made it increasingly inefficient for me to manually consolidate data from the different channels and sources. To put it frankly, it was a pain every quarter and not something I wanted to do. If I hadn't been able to automate much if not most of the process and then just do minimal work to actually produce the executive reports, I'm not sure I would have done it, or perhaps not as frequently.

THE NEW RULES NOW INCLUDE MARKETING DATA ANALYTICS

These days you cannot swing a cat without hitting someone talking about the importance of data – from analytics and data warehouses to metrics and intelligence. One of the biggest consequences of the digital transformation was a massive uptick in the amount of information that we as marketers could collect about buyer behavior, not just after they become a customer, but from the first moment they search for us online and hopefully every step along the way to becoming a customer.

In 2007, David Meerman Scott (who wrote the thought-provoking foreword to *Data-First Marketing*) published his groundbreaking book, *The New Rules of Marketing and PR*. An enduring success that has evolved as digital marketing has grown, David's book recently released a seventh edition and today is published in 29 languages. Looking back to when it first came out, however, we now understand that this book was documenting the beginning of a digital marketing revolution, fueled by the initial explosion of digital technologies in the Age of Discovery and adoption of the surviving technologies that could be monetized in the Age of Reckoning. By 2007, digital technology – from the World Wide Web to search engines to digital advertising platforms – had matured enough and gained enough widespread business adoption to begin to completely transform what was possible when it came to marketing. Digital was an entirely new frontier with a tantalizingly new and, more importantly, attainable promise: to be able to reach potential customers with exactly what they were looking for, exactly when they were looking for it.

But no one ever said it would be easy.

The explosion of martech is important to understand because it mirrors and fuels the rapid change and growth of what is expected of marketers; there are entirely new digital channels to explore, new technologies and skillsets to master and integrate, and a mountain of data to collect, analyze, and utilize. Traditional marketing isn't dead; rather digital marketing has transformed our discipline into something more, something better, and something both easier and harder at the same time.

B2C companies, in particular, understand the very different reality of how they must compete today, with more buyer behavior and signaling information than ever before available via social media and in the data they can capture themselves along each buyer's journey. This explosion of customer data along with the growth and availability of big data technologies have changed the priorities for B2C marketers – to own the customer experience and master customer data in order to be able to quickly react to changing customer sentiment and personalize messages and experience for each customer. Currently, case studies and research on marketing data analytics tend to focus on B2C companies and how they are utilizing data analytics and data-driven marketing in their organizations:

> There are now major disparities in performance between a small group of technology leaders and the average company – in some cases creating winner-take-most dynamics. The leading global "unicorns" tend to be companies with business models predicated on data and analytics, such as Uber, Lyft, Didi Chuxing, Palantir, Flipkart, Airbnb, DJI, Snapchat, Pinterest, BlablaCar, and Spotify. These companies differentiate themselves through their data and analytics assets, processes, and strategies. (MGI, 2016, p. 6)

But while B2C companies might agree that data-driven marketing is a priority, actual adoption has been slower than expected. Even the Fortune 1000 companies employing data scientist teams and big data and AI tools have not fully utilized all of this data for meaningful business insights. In 2016, McKinsey published a report, "The Age of Analytics: Competing in a Data-Driven World." The information and examples come from Fortune 1000 companies and although the outlook was positive, there was still a lot of room to grow:

> ...many companies that have begun to deploy data and analytics have not realized the full value. Some have responded to competitive pressure by making large technology investments but have failed to make the organizational changes needed to make the most of them. An effective transformation strategy

can be broken down into several components. The first step should be asking some fundamental questions to shape the strategic vision: What will data and analytics be used for? How will the insights drive value? How will the value be measured? (MGI 2016, p. 4)

These are the fundamental questions every company, big or small, should be asking themselves as they work to make their data-driven visions a reality.

Making the Shift to Data-First Marketing

When it comes to data-driven marketing in business-to-business (B2B) companies, adoption has been even slower, but the opportunity is tremendous. Marketing data – from buyer behavior to statistics on marketing campaign effectiveness and ROI – is already available to B2B marketers in various martech platforms they are using or can be made readily available with some changes to data collection and integration efforts tied to each company's key performance indicators (KPIs), yet most B2B marketing teams do not take advantage of this information. Data-first marketing is the shift to thinking about data in strategic ways and incorporating this in marketing's day-to-day activities.

This starts with marketing leadership – CMOs and heads of marketing – driving the data-first marketing charge by explaining to the business just what can be achieved with this new mindset, co-opting key stakeholders like the CEO and other C-suite executives and the sales team and resetting expectations about marketing goals, value, and ROI that can be shown using actual data. This also requires marketing leadership to retrain and retain or hire marketing staff with the right skillsets who can adopt the data-first mindset, along with adapting marketing processes like campaign execution so that they support data-first goals and deliverables.

We have many ideas about why the promise of digital marketing and the reality of what marketers do today are so far apart in organizations, based on our actual experiences with companies in a variety of industries. But in the end, what it comes down to is that most marketers don't know where to start or have a clear path of how to get from A to Z.

In this book, we explore what is necessary to bridge the gap between where marketing is and where the business needs marketing to be by adopting data-first marketing principles. More specifically, we provide a Data-First Marketing Campaign Framework: an accessible, repeatable process, embraced by the entire organization, that starts with business goals and ends with campaign and asset data analytics that feed back into the next campaign iteration to create a culture of continuous improvement. We will lay out the steps involved to transform your organization using data-first marketing and how to tailor them to each organization. The marketing fundamentals haven't changed (e.g., the four Ps of product, price, placement, promotion), but how we need to use them to take advantage of the opportunities that digital marketing, martech, and data make possible absolutely has.

CHAPTER 2

Data Levels the Playing Field: Lessons from Moneyball

If you pay attention to the world around you, it's not hard to understand that we live in the Age of Analytics now. Technology and the digital economy have resulted in an explosion of data that is being used in every industry around us, to greater and lesser extents.

Sports analytics is an industry standard for professional sports worldwide. Every major tennis tournament highlights interesting statistics and even predictive analytics, and the top players – who can afford it – pay six figures to teams of data analysts to give them a competitive edge (Briggs, 2019). Formula One (F1) racing embraces data analytics, embedding over a hundred sensors on each car to generate 3GB of data and 1,500 data points per second during races (Amazon, 2018) – all of which is analyzed to develop winning strategies overall and to make incremental improvements to the cars themselves that can shave critical seconds off of racing times over the course of an F1 season. Analytics, and the ability to invest in it, makes such a difference that F1 is instituting cost caps on things like car development to offset the huge advantages that the richest teams have over the poorest; such advantages currently translate to winning every race (Edelstein, 2019). Even curling is getting into the act, facilitated by sites like curlingzone.com which started by collecting years' worth of curling line scores and eventually developed an "analytics offering used by both 2018 Olympic Gold medalists," as described on the 2019 MIT Sports Analytics Conference website.

As marketers, we read all the time about the importance of marketing analytics, usually about Fortune 1000 companies using it to better understand their customer bases in order to personalize experiences, better engage potential buyers, and build customer loyalty. These companies generate billions of dollars in revenue every year; at an average of 10.5% of revenue (if we use the number from the 2019–2020 Gartner marketing spend survey), their annual marketing budgets range from about $2 billion to over $50 billion.

This kind of spending power enables them to purchase specialized martech and personnel to power their data-driven marketing initiatives – purchases that are out of reach for most of us. For example, these are the companies that can afford to invest in customer data platforms (CDPs) to get a unified view of demographic, behavioral, and transactional customer data for marketers. According to Gartner, the typical cost to purchase and implement a CDP is anywhere from $100K to $300K annually, and that cost can be significantly higher if the CDP is homegrown.

These are also the companies with outsized marketing budgets who can afford to engage teams of data analysts/scientists either as consultants or as employees to glean insights from all of that very expensive collected data. Given their advantages, they should be the precursors for the rest of us – examples of what we should strive for when it comes to shifting to data-driven marketing. Yet it seems like size has its disadvantages as well. Change is especially difficult for large organizations, and since digital marketing first disrupted how classic marketing operated almost 20 years ago now, there has been no bigger opportunity and challenge for marketers to seize and conquer than now, with data in the Age of Analytics.

Insights and analytics have appeared on the CMO priority list for years, with good reason: 76% of marketing leaders say they use data and analytics to drive key decisions. Yet marketing organizations also struggle to evolve their data capabilities. (Starita, 2019).

Instead of being a competitive disadvantage, data analytics can actually go a long way toward creating a more even playing field for the rest of us. In some ways, being smaller can actually be an advantage when it comes to the true transformation required to adopt the data-first marketing mentality that we set out in this book. To explain why and how, we only have to look at how analytics have been adopted in the seemingly unrelated field of baseball.

THE MONEYBALL DATA-FIRST PHILOSOPHY

The best example is the spark that lit the sports analytics fire and has done the most to popularize analytics to a wider audience. The book *Moneyball: The Art of Winning an Unfair Game,* by Michael Lewis, was published in 2003; the movie adapted from it came out in 2011. This groundbreaking work clearly lays out a new, data-driven strategy defined by Billy Beane, the general manager (GM) of the Oakland Athletics (A's) and supported by analytics work from Paul DePodesta, assistant GM. The A's had a problem that sounds very familiar to most of us: they had to find a way to compete and win against teams that had significantly more money.

Moneyball is educational for marketers and anyone who can understand that data insights can be transformative; its impact can be seen in a variety of industries, from government to business. In the book, the A's had to be smarter about how they spent the smaller pot they had to build a winning team. By relying on data and doing deep dives into the statistics to understand which metrics were really meaningful (spoiler – not the ones that everyone had believed in for almost 150 years) and then acting upon that intelligence, the A's ended up revolutionizing MLB offense. By 2013, more than 75% of MLB teams were using this data-driven strategy, specifically called sabermetrics, defined by Bill James in 1980 as "the search for objective knowledge about baseball," mainly through application of statistical analysis, and described extensively in the book. And as we showed, data-driven decision-making is not confined just to baseball. By 2018, "every major professional sports team either has an analytics department or an analytics expert on staff (Steinberg, 2015)."

Necessity is the mother of invention. The A's were at a severe disadvantage, and it caused them to think outside of the box for answers. Right around the time that the A's were changing how they operated, the Report of the Independent Members of the Commissioner's

Blue Ribbon Panel on Baseball Economics was released. The report reinforced the growing sentiment at the time that revenue disparities among the MLB teams had led to chronic competitive imbalance, which seemed to be getting worse. In 1990, the gap between the top and bottom payrolls was $14.3 million; by 2000, the gap was $77.3 million (Haupert and Winter, 2018).

Conventional baseball wisdom and common sense said that teams with more money win because they can buy the best talent. In order to compete, the A's created a new offensive strategy driven by data and not convention. The results in 2002 were a record-breaking 20-game winning streak and overall winning season that helped them make division playoffs that year.

Billy Beane and Paul DePodesta took advantage of necessity and opportunity to reinvent how ballplayers were evaluated for the draft. On one side were the veteran scouts, who had played baseball, some of them briefly in the major league and most of them topping out in the minor leagues. For the most part, they represented conventional scouting wisdom, which relied on what they could see; their experienced eyes judged a player on certain agreed-upon physical criteria that everyone used. On the other side were the Harvard economics grads who might have never played baseball and Billy Beane, once a promising high school player who had never reached the superstar potential many of those old scouts thought he should have achieved. Beane and DePodesta had never even seen many of the players they would eventually select but they had access to extensive player stats and wanted to retrain their scouts to embrace "performance scouting," previously an insult in scouting circles.

This is a simplification of the old and the new, but it sets up the tension between the way things were "always" done and the new way things should be. At one point, Billy Beane asks the most experienced scout, Dick Bogard, if performance scouting made sense to him:

> "Oh definitely," says Bogie, motioning to Paul's computer. "It's a new game. Years ago we didn't have these stats to look up. We had to go with what we saw." (Lewis, 2003, p. 39)

Embracing performance scouting opened up opportunities for the A's that no other team, entrenched in the old way of scouting, could even understand. When it came to trades in particular, the A's knew they couldn't compete when it came to grabbing the obvious talent that everyone could see and covet, so they maximized their bargain-hunting by mostly going after players who looked flawed – overweight, slow, injured – but when it came to the metrics that mattered to the team, these players were exactly who they were seeking. In this case, being the underdog was actually an advantage because it made the A's buck tradition to create competitive advantage.

It seems like a no-brainer that data should help to drive player selection, but it still took years for the other MLB teams to adopt. It required a major shift in mindset from how baseball had worked since the nineteenth century – not just to employ a data analyst to crunch the numbers that could help make personnel decisions, but to truly institutionalize a data-first strategy that drove which players even made the lineup in each game. Data-first created a system that the A's religiously followed in spite of individual losses because the goal was broader – a target number of wins over the entire season in order to make it to the playoffs.

Moneyball offers many lessons for marketers today, but especially for those in small to midsize enterprises as they transition to the next level of data-driven marketing as we define it: data-first marketing. By necessity, the A's did not take a gradual approach to their new strategy; Billy Beane and Paul DePodesta drove the transformation from the top down and ensured compliance by retraining managers and hand-selecting players who had the skills and attributes that the team needed overall. Committing to data-first is critical to the success of your own transformation.

LESSON 1: DEFY CONVENTION, USING DATA

The term "data-driven marketing" has been around for several years now, but wholescale adoption is still elusive, even by the very largest companies. In the 2015–2016 CMO Spend Survey, Gartner announced that "digital marketing has moved into the mainstream," meaning that instead of being treated as separate, digital marketing tactics were "merging into the larger marketing operation," mainly as a driver for growth and innovation. By the 2018–2019 CMO Spend Survey, marketing technology spend topped the other options at 29% of the marketing budget, compared to labor, agency, and media costs, and 9.2% was being spent on marketing analytics (Pemberton, 2018).

Yet, despite this commitment to martech and analytics, the same Gartner 2018 Marketing Analytics Survey showed that the expensive data scientists they employed were wasting time performing basic activities in more than 45% of marketing organizations and over half of those surveyed had limited trust in the modeling techniques being employed. Gartner surveyed five hundred "marketing analytics leaders" to get these findings; translated that means these numbers come from very large companies with very large marketing budgets. Good news for those of us who cannot spend $5 million or more on marketing analytics: the large companies haven't gotten it right yet either.

In this case, smaller definitely means nimbler and an opportunity for companies to create competitive advantage by adopting a data-first marketing strategy; the next level of data-driven marketing still remains primarily tactical for most companies. Even with far larger budgets to spend on technology and data scientists, the "marketing analytics leaders" are struggling to make their investments pay off. We posit that one of the major reasons for this is because they treat analytics like a band-aid on top of current marketing operations. Smaller marketing teams have a much better chance to truly transform themselves, from top to bottom, to incorporate data-first thinking in every stage of marketing – including setting goals, defining metrics, conducting testing, and reporting on ROI.

David versus Goliaths: Winning Using Data-Driven Digital Marketing

Working in a technology startup as digital marketing took off was like being in a perfect storm. The growth of websites, SEO, digital advertising, and marketing automation in the 2000s could not have been better timing for us. ScienceLogic competitors were huge blue-chip companies: IBM, CA, HP, Microsoft; they were well established in the network monitoring market, and in fact they were the industry standards. Combined, they owned an overwhelming majority of the multibillion-dollar market, and most customers were still paying their high maintenance costs many years after the initial purchase. How was a startup supposed to break into this little club? If you bought from HP, you never had to justify your purchase. Conversely, if you bought from ScienceLogic, you definitely had to justify your purchase, and in some cases, you continued to pay the maintenance costs for HP, which you still "owned" but literally kept in the closet.

Digital marketing in its nascency was a boon for the smaller company marketer. In many ways, it leveled the playing field. To a certain extent, it didn't matter how big you actually were on the web; it only mattered how big and how reputable you appeared. Applying SEO and digital advertising, we could appear right next to the search listings and ads of these much bigger players and even borrow a bit of their legitimacy. First-mover advantages definitely applied. We began to optimize for cloud computing monitoring keywords in 2009, long before "the cloud" became something everyone knew because we believed even then that it would be big, and we were proven right. We soon grabbed the number one rankings for those keywords in Google search when the search volume for them was barely anything and retained top 10 or first-page rankings even after they became very competitive terms in SEO. We also used LinkedIn advertising in its early stages and took advantage of lower costs and relative lower competition (compared to the costs on the more mature Google AdWords platform) and the ability to target based on company, title, self-designated groups and more, resulting in over 200% more leads than Google AdWords provided while spending 82% less budget. Our marketing budget was a drop in the bucket compared to our large competitors, but we used it judiciously, and only in areas where we could get the best ROI, and digital, with its wealth of available data, allowed us to track leads all the way through to sales. No Super Bowl ads for us – our money was pretty strictly spent on lead generation, which equaled revenue generation, and not on general branding awareness, which could not be measured.

Don't be afraid to question the status quo and try something new, especially if the data supports you.

LESSON 2: YOU MAY NOT WIN THE WORLD SERIES, BUT YOU CAN BE A CONTENDER

Using the "Moneyball" strategy put in place by Billy Beane and Paul DePodesta, the Oakland A's made the American League Division playoffs multiple times but only won them one time. They have yet to win a World Series. Is this a failure of strategy?

Since 2002, the Oakland A's have had more winning seasons than losing ones and have placed first or second in the American League 11 times. That's a win in any book, especially if viewed through the lens of conventional baseball wisdom, which said that teams needed to buy their way to winning.

Similar to digital marketing in its earlier days, marketing analytics provides the same kind of opportunities to create competitive advantages for the marketers who can get it right quickly. There's a window of opportunity right now, where smaller companies can use the intelligence and efficiencies that marketing analytics can provide in order to effectively compete with much larger competitors.

Making smarter decisions, based on data, can accelerate your growth and make smaller companies in particular look much bigger than you actually are. The key here is to understand that for smaller and new players, you may never have number one (or two or three) market share, but number four or five or six can still get you a "seat at the table." At ScienceLogic, for example, we had the goal to be on the network (and later cloud) monitoring shortlist for potential buyers, which translated to sales because we could be included in important RFPs. Digital marketing combined with a rigorous adherence to pursue activities and campaigns with the best ROI helped us to achieve that.

LESSON 3: ALWAYS ASK "WHY?"

The box score, invented in 1845 and then improved by sportswriter Henry Chadwick in 1859, records the significant events in a baseball game that contributed to winning or losing. Despite changes over the years, it is still used today and basically what you see in the corner of your television if you tune into a game. By the time Bill James came along in 1977 and published his first Baseball Abstract, one of the major things that he questioned was the accuracy of the box score metrics to describe why a team won or lost.

> "I am a mechanic with numbers," he wrote to readers of the third Abstract, "tinkering with the records of baseball games to see how the machinery of the baseball offense works. I do not start with the numbers any more than a mechanic starts with a monkey wrench. I start with the game, with the things that I see there and the things that people say there. And I ask: Is it true? Can you validate it? Can you measure it? How does it fit with the rest of the machinery? And for those answers I go to the record books.... What is remarkable to me is that I have so little company. Baseball keeps copious records, and people talk about them and argue about them and think about them a great deal. Why doesn't anybody use them? Why doesn't anybody say, in the face of this contention or that one, 'Prove it'?" (Lewis, 2003, p. 75)

James questioned all the traditional metrics. By running analyses on tens of thousands of baseball stats that he had laboriously collected himself, and then on even more collected by businesses that were created to fill this growing need, he discovered that the ones being used in the box score did not paint the right picture. Using a scientific method, he disproved the value of several metrics that had been institutionalized in baseball as something "everyone knew" led to winning games. *Stolen bases are important. Sometimes you need to sacrifice yourself. It's better to slug away at a ball than draw a walk (in fact a "walk" was counted as an "error" in Chadwick's box score). High batting average teams win.* In fact, James proved that all of these were false. Later, Pete Palmer and Dick Cramer, statisticians working in the footsteps of James, came up with two stats that did matter statistically – on base percentage and slugging (OPS), which are what the Oakland A's used when evaluating the value of players they were recruiting and trading, and by being the first to use them, they gained a distinct winning advantage over the rest of the field.

When you read about this, you can't help but think, "Of course. That makes sense." Yet what was interesting is that while he was publishing the Baseball Abstract (1977–1984), the biggest readership was baseball fans and not baseball professionals. Most baseball managers discounted it, with a notable exception being a certain Oakland A's GM who would become Billy Beane's boss. Even after *Moneyball* was published, the backlash was severe, as if the thought of using data to drive decisions about baseball offense was an insult to everything and everyone that came before.

Let's look at some metrics in marketing that fall into the same category – metrics that are still being used because they have always been used but don't actually contribute to "winning" (i.e., sales/revenue). Two come to mind immediately: email open rate and website traffic.

Now there may be exceptions to lumping these metrics in the "old and useless" category; for example, maybe your website gets paid for additional traffic via advertising, but these are two metrics that you should question: "Why are they important?"

Email open rate has been around on email reporting since the beginning, even though how it is measured has changed over the years. Specifically, every email client is different, plus there are the technical difficulties of measuring on mobile versus desktop, which has muddled the measurement so much that some of us stopped paying a lot of attention to it years ago, yet it persists on every out-of-the-box email performance report, and often it's even the first metric listed. Why? Because it's always been there, so people still expect it to be there? By comparison, click-through rate is a much more important number because it shows actual engagement with your recipient; just because an email is "opened" does not mean it was actually read by anyone. Literally, it could mean that it was just the next email in someone's inbox that immediately got deleted. If you google "email open rate," you will see many listings of companies wanting to help you improve it, but very few that talk about the issues surrounding it.

Website traffic is a very interesting stat because more than any other it seems like a vanity metric for most people: it looks good but doesn't necessarily mean anything useful for the business. Usually this is a large number, and the thinking is that it makes your marketing team somehow look better to be able to share it; it sounds impressive when you can tell the CEO, "Our web traffic is up this month. We had XX thousand/million visitors this month." Yes, and? In a lot of ways, it's very similar to email open rate – a metric that has been around from the beginning, usually one of the first things you see in Google Analytics, but what does it really mean for your business? As a marketer, I do keep track of this number just to see if there are any big dips or a trend that I need to take a closer look at, but I would not point this out as an achievement unless it is a specific goal for the business.

So why do marketers still use these metrics on the reports and dashboards that show how their campaigns and programs are doing? Before you show any metric to the CEO and CFO, you need to ask, "Why does that matter?" because if you think they wouldn't ask the same question, you're only fooling yourself, and perhaps only in the short-term.

Everyone likes an underdog, maybe even Yankees fans. Done right, data analytics has the possibility to dramatically improve your marketing campaigns, which helps you to compete better. And if you've aligned them with business goals, they should help the company overall to gain more customers, provide better customer experiences, increase customer loyalty, and boost pipeline and revenue – whatever your specific business goals may be. Large or small, every company must move in this direction. If you're a large company and you don't do it, you risk being passed. If you're a smaller company and you do it, you only have room to grow.

CHAPTER 3

Data-First Marketing: Transforming Your Marketing Organization

Increasingly, data-driven or data-based marketing is the topic of discussion for marketers. This seems straightforward – that marketers would use information they have collected to develop strategies and make better decisions about content, campaigns, and the like. But most companies, even the marketing "leaders" with the resources to truly invest in data analytics resources and capabilities, are not realizing the full potential of the data and intelligence available to them. Too often, data-driven marketing is still considered an "add-on," utilizing data analysis resources residing outside of the marketing function instead of being used every day by marketers themselves. Most data-driven marketing is reactive and not strategic – applied after campaigns are executed instead of being incorporated from the beginning of setting strategy and goals. It's a nice-to-have instead of a must-have. It's no wonder that data-driven marketing is still marginalized.

In order for data-driven marketing to succeed in any organization, there must be a fundamental transformation of the marketing function. We are asking marketers to embrace something that most of them have never done before. You can't just say, "We're going to start analyzing our data to make smarter decisions." You need to set your marketing team up for success and change your culture to one where you think of data first, not last, which is exactly where data-first marketing comes in.

WHAT IS DATA-FIRST MARKETING?

Data-first marketing is a new marketing strategy that focuses on intelligently utilizing the vast amount of marketing data available today in order to create true competitive advantage in any industry. It combines data-driven marketing with business strategy and goals and requires a top-down transformation of people, processes, technology, data, and culture.

First and foremost, data-first marketing is strategic and requires a transformation of mindset and skillset by marketers and the business; it is rooted in marketing experience and takes advantage of current digital marketing and martech opportunities that require marketing to be fully invested to succeed.

Adoption of data-driven marketing for business-to-consumer (B2C) companies is well documented, and the further it develops with the aid of big data and artificial intelligence, the more data-driven marketing in the B2C sphere will change from a unique competitive advantage into a requirement to compete.

Adoption in the business-to-business (B2B) space, however, has been slower due to a variety of factors, including budget constraints, lack of data, scarcity of skills, and more. The growing maturation of marketing technology tools for ROI reporting, attribution, and marketing intelligence that can be used by all make this the perfect time for the early adopters in the B2B marketing space to take advantage. In the last year alone, the acquisitions in the analytics/visualization market are huge signals that the entire market is headed in this direction; Salesforce bought Tableau for $15.7B, and Google bought Looker for $2.6B.

Marketing data analytics is the new battleground for marketers today. The early adopters will help their businesses compete and win. This translates to true value that, because of the data it is predicated on, can be shown clearly to the CEO and other stakeholders of the C-suite. Adopting data-first marketing not only positions marketers for success now, but also develops valuable skills that are scarce and will be increasingly sought after in the job market as all companies will go down this path.

WHY DATA-FIRST MARKETING?

Most data-driven marketing, as executed today, does not go far enough. Done right, this is a fundamental change to the marketing function – from setting strategy and goals to actual execution. Data-first marketing embodies this change, taking data-driven marketing to the next level. In order to achieve this, data-first marketing:

- Conveys the importance of data to marketers today. No one thing has more potential to impact our marketing efforts and marketing ROI, for better or for worse. Data – and more specifically, deriving intelligence from data – can create true competitive advantage for businesses, and, conversely, not being able to use it effectively when everyone else is focusing on that can put a business at a competitive disadvantage.
- Is a mindset. It is a reminder to marketers that they need to start thinking about how to produce, collect, integrate, and analyze data from all campaigns and across all channels from the very beginning of the planning phase. All campaigns should always be aligned, not just to marketing goals, but to business goals and strategy, and the only way to prove marketing value relative to business goals and strategy is through data.
- Emphasizes a drastically different approach to day-to-day marketing operations, where results residing in the data are open and transparent and should be built upon to improve for the next campaign, the one after that, and so on, in an iterative process that makes marketing organizations stronger, better, and faster.

WHY ISN'T MARKETING ALREADY DOING THIS?

If everyone "knows" that they should be moving to a data-driven model to make smarter decisions faster, then why aren't they doing it? We covered some of this in Chapter 2 ("Lessons from Moneyball"); people default to doing what they've always done, especially if everyone else seems to be doing it that way as well. Most marketers answer "what" and "how many" but tend not to answer "why," which we also brought up when talking about volume versus value metrics in Chapter 1. From our own experiences in marketing departments and working with client marketing teams in a variety of industries, we have found two additional obstacles that any marketer will understand and commiserate with.

You're Too Busy

Marketing teams are consumed with adopting new martech. It's a never-ending cycle. As referenced earlier, the martech landscape is growing exponentially, and the fear is that if you don't keep up, you will be left behind. Beyond the fact that martech can open up new channels, markets, and segments, just keeping up with the changes to your existing martech or replacing existing infrastructure for the newest and the "best" and having to learn completely new systems can be a full-time job. Marketing is so buried in making sure you can execute that taking the time to stop and strategize and then ensure you're keeping to that strategy is taking second place – if you ever even have the time to get there.

And the martech that is supposed to help can even be the source of the problem. Recently, at our own company we evaluated replacement marketing automation tools. Of particular interest was each tool's reporting capabilities, of course. There was a myriad of questions to consider and how they would impact our measurement and our team during implementation:

- Would we be able to get the marketing ROI reporting that we currently had?
- How specifically would we do that across how many of our martech systems?
- Would we need to tie into the CRM in order to get to the business-relevant marketing metrics or could we actually pull all the metrics we needed out of one system?

To determine the answers, we turned to the salesperson about the tool's out-of-the-box ROI report.

Us:	*How does lead source get set in this ROI report? Is that first- or last-touch attribution or manually set?*
Salesperson:	*I think it's first-touch.*
Us:	*Is there any way to modify this for multi-touch attribution?*
Salesperson:	*Our customers just want first-touch attribution.*

Really? With all the work that marketing does to "touch" prospects multiple times, in different ways, in the effort to keep them interested, keep you and your products/services top of mind, and hopefully to convert them to customers, you'd only want the first campaign you hit them with to get any kind of credit for business ROI? This is simply not true. Okay, so we understand that this is a salesperson trying to get past any possible objections we might have had (in case you're interested, we did not choose that tool), but it illuminates yet another problem with martech.

We have no doubt that many marketing teams rely on these out-of-the-box reports. For some, it's a matter of time and convenience. For others, it's the second point to make. . . .

It's Hard

The sheer work involved in navigating, customizing, and integrating what is most likely multiple martech systems to get to the reporting that you need for your business is completely daunting – you don't even know where to start and/or you don't have the skills in-house to get it done. And in the meantime, you have another three campaigns to get out in the next week.

Out-of-the box performance and ROI reports are good enough, aren't they? When it comes to data-first marketing, the answer is no. Every business is unique; your goals are unique, the competitive environment you operate in is unique, your assets are unique (you created them!), the metrics that move the needle for your sales and marketing engine are unique. Without customization, if that's even possible, out-of-the-box reports cannot give you the complete and unique picture you need to use your own data to improve marketing performance and efficiency. If the point is to use data analytics to create competitive advantage, why would you rely on a report that anyone, including your competitors, can produce easily? If you had the time and skills to change it, of course you would, and we hope to give you some specific tips on how to do that in Part II of this book.

But until you can make this change, if you bring these reports to your next executive meeting, be prepared to back up what they say when the CEO questions it, and increasingly, the CEO is questioning it.

BEGINNING THE TRANSFORMATION

Data-first marketing transformation touches all aspects of the marketing organization, from people, processes and technologies to data strategy and governance and overall organizational culture (see Figure 3.1). It requires fundamental changes to the way most marketing teams operate, the marketing technology they are using, and even what skills marketers should be developing.

Embracing data-first marketing starts with defining and aligning marketing goals with business goals and ensuring that key stakeholders like sales and the CEO are on the same page. Once goals are defined, you then need to agree upon the metrics or KPIs that will show marketing campaign performance against these goals and set up how and where this data will be captured. If you need sales to input data that will later be used in the reports or dashboards you use to visualize the KPIs, then you might need to modify sales processes to get the data you need. In order to get to the KPIs and do meaningful analysis, some of your data may reside in different data stores you need to access or there may be some level of integration necessary. When you set up the campaign, you must ensure that any data you

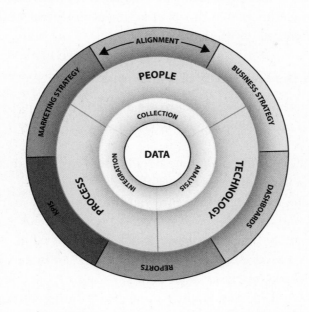

FIGURE 3.1   Data-First Marketing Framework.

need from the campaign execution itself will be captured in a format that you can use and access. This might mean creating new database fields, and you will need to define how that data is used going forward and communicate that to anyone (e.g., sales, operations, etc.) who might need to know. Depending on the campaign and channel, you might need to use a new martech platform entirely (e.g., a new webinar platform), in which case, one of the criteria you use to assess the platform should be if and how you can access the data you think you will need based upon the campaign, the KPIs, and the agreed upon goals. Can you create the reports and dashboards you need from that data, or should you integrate that platform with an existing visualization tool?

This is just a sample of what having a data-first marketing mindset means for daily marketing activities. As you can see, the imperative here is to think about the data you will need to capture, analyze, and visualize down the road to show marketing performance – and all the details that go along with that.

Looking at the Five Steps of Transformation

Part II of this book goes into more detail on the five steps to data-first marketing transformation that we have described above:

1. Marketing-Business Alignment: aligning with key stakeholders and agreeing on metrics that matter
2. Data Integration, Architecture, and Technical Resources: data strategy and data governance across the martech stack and beyond
3. Data Analysis: how to analyze the data to derive value
4. Data-First Marketing Campaign Framework: embracing data-first in daily marketing tasks
5. Data-First Marketing Staffing and Culture: hiring, retraining, and developing a data-first culture

Remember, the goal here is continuous improvement. Data-first marketing transformation is not something that happens overnight or once and you're done. Ensuring that marketing goals are tied to business goals should happen not one time, but every time. Defining data strategy evolves as the needs of the business change, and evaluating martech, setting up the platform/tools, and integrating data to support that strategy are constant activities, as is analyzing the data produced from the platforms/tools and predefined processes. Marketing staff need to be trained or retrained until data and analysis is the first thing they think of, rather than the last or not at all, and the Data-First Marketing Campaign Framework can help by guiding staff in daily marketing operations that embrace the new data-first culture.

But first up in Part II is a self-assessment. We introduce a Data-First Marketing Maturity Model, and your answers to the assessment can help to pinpoint where your company is and, equally important, where you would like to be.

PART

Transforming Your Organization: Adopting Data-First Marketing

CHAPTER 4

Assessing Your Organization's Marketing Maturity Level

In part two of this book, we'll address how to create a data-first marketing organization. To understand what work you'll need to focus on requires first assessing where your marketing organization currently falls on the data-first maturity model, as shown in Figure 4.1. Where is your organization today? Where do you want to be a year from now?

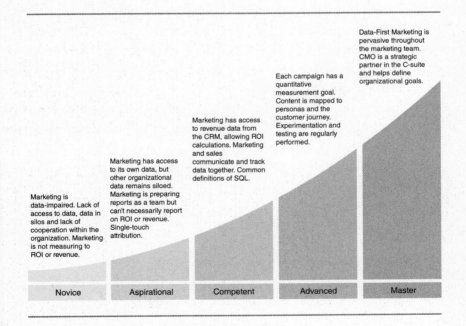

FIGURE 4.1 **The Data-First Marketing Maturity Model.**

Completing the data-first marketing assessment will help to identify areas of improvement. The second part of this book then takes you through the steps in more detail to complete a data-first marketing transformation.

The data-first marketing assessment is broken into five segments. Rate your agreement with each statement and tally your score at the end. You may note that answers C, D, and E each have zero points. This was done intentionally to weight each question as each pertains to the data-first maturity model levels. Even though these answers have the same score, answer as honestly as you can for each question because the answers will help you evaluate which of the following chapters may provide the most insight for growth.

1. ALIGNING MARKETING WITH THE BUSINESS

1. Marketing is perceived as a revenue center (as opposed to a cost center) in our company.
   a. Highly agree (5)
   b. Somewhat agree (3)
   c. Not sure (0)
   d. Somewhat disagree (0)
   e. Highly disagree (0)
2. Marketing is viewed by the entire organization as providing a high degree of value to the business.
   a. Highly agree (5)
   b. Somewhat agree (3)
   c. Not sure (0)
   d. Somewhat disagree (0)
   e. Highly disagree (0)
3. Marketing strategy is aligned with/built from business strategy.
   a. Highly agree (5)
   b. Somewhat agree (3)
   c. Not sure (0)
   d. Somewhat disagree (0)
   e. Highly disagree (0)

4. Marketing clearly aligns its objectives and goals with the company's objectives and goals.
   a. Highly agree (5)
   b. Somewhat agree (3)
   c. Not sure (0)
   d. Somewhat disagree (0)
   e. Highly disagree (0)
5. Marketing and sales are strongly aligned.
   a. Highly agree (5)
   b. Somewhat agree (3)
   c. Not sure (0)
   d. Somewhat disagree (0)
   e. Highly disagree (0)
6. There is a clear definition of a Marketing Qualified Lead (MQL).
   a. Highly agree (5)
   b. Somewhat agree (3)
   c. Not sure (0)
   d. Somewhat disagree (0)
   e. Highly disagree (0)
7. There is a clear definition of a Sales Qualified Lead (SQL).
   a. Highly agree (5)
   b. Somewhat agree (3)
   c. Not sure (0)
   d. Somewhat disagree (0)
   e. Highly disagree (0)
8. The sales team shares agreement on the Sales Qualified Lead (SQL) definition.
   a. Highly agree (5)
   b. Somewhat agree (3)
   c. Not sure (0)
   d. Somewhat disagree (0)
   e. Highly disagree (0)
9. The marketing team works directly with sales to define accounts to target.
   a. Highly agree (5)

b. Somewhat agree (3)

c. Not sure (0)

d. Somewhat disagree (0)

e. Highly disagree (0)

10. Marketing leadership actively seeks input from sales leadership when developing marketing strategy.
    a. Highly agree (5)
    b. Somewhat agree (3)
    c. Not sure (0)
    d. Somewhat disagree (0)
    e. Highly disagree (0)

11. Marketing has access to the sales data we need to report on opportunities and closed deals.
    a. Highly agree (5)
    b. Somewhat agree (3)
    c. Not sure (0)
    d. Somewhat disagree (0)
    e. Highly disagree (0)

12. I have a high degree of confidence in the accuracy of sales data.
    a. Highly agree (5)
    b. Somewhat agree (3)
    c. Not sure (0)
    d. Somewhat disagree (0)
    e. Highly disagree (0)

2. ARCHITECTURE AND TECHNICAL RESOURCES

13. Marketing has a clear understanding of what systems contain the data we need for reporting.
    a. Highly agree (5)
    b. Somewhat agree (3)
    c. Not sure (0)
    d. Somewhat disagree (0)
    e. Highly disagree (0)

14. Marketing has access to the systems that contain the data we need for reporting.
    a. Highly agree (5)
    b. Somewhat agree (3)
    c. Not sure (0)
    d. Somewhat disagree (0)
    e. Highly disagree (0)
15. Marketing is able to confidently and concretely report on ROI.
    a. Highly agree (5)
    b. Somewhat agree (3)
    c. Not sure (0)
    d. Somewhat disagree (0)
    e. Highly disagree (0)
16. Our martech stack is fully integrated.
    a. Highly agree (5)
    b. Somewhat agree (3)
    c. Not sure (0)
    d. Somewhat disagree (0)
    e. Highly disagree (0)
17. The data we need for marketing reporting to revenue and ROI are accessible through one platform, such as a dashboard.
    a. Highly agree (5)
    b. Somewhat agree (3)
    c. Not sure (0)
    d. Somewhat disagree (0)
    e. Highly disagree (0)
18. We share and present our data to others in the C-suite.
    a. Highly agree (5)
    b. Somewhat agree (3)
    c. Not sure (0)
    d. Somewhat disagree (0)
    e. Highly disagree (0)
19. We create charts to communicate data to the C-suite.
    a. Highly agree (5)
    b. Somewhat agree (3)

c. Not sure (0)

d. Somewhat disagree (0)

e. Highly disagree (0)

3. ANALYZING DATA

20. I have a high degree of confidence in the marketing team's ability to collect and analyze marketing data correctly.
    a. Highly agree (5)
    b. Somewhat agree (3)
    c. Not sure (0)
    d. Somewhat disagree (0)
    e. Highly disagree (0)
21. We have a well-defined marketing funnel or stages of the buyer's journey.
    a. Highly agree (5)
    b. Somewhat agree (3)
    c. Not sure (0)
    d. Somewhat disagree (0)
    e. Highly disagree (0)
22. I have a high degree of confidence that we are measuring the correct data on the path to ROI and revenue.
    a. Highly agree (5)
    b. Somewhat agree (3)
    c. Not sure (0)
    d. Somewhat disagree (0)
    e. Highly disagree (0)
23. We use marketing data to improve our efficiency and performance of our campaigns.
    a. Highly agree (5)
    b. Somewhat agree (3)
    c. Not sure (0)
    d. Somewhat disagree (0)
    e. Highly disagree (0)

24. We have data expert resources either in-house or externally that help us analyze our data.
    a. Highly agree (5)
    b. Somewhat agree (3)
    c. Not sure (0)
    d. Somewhat disagree (0)
    e. Highly disagree (0)

4. CAMPAIGN FRAMEWORK

25. Our marketing team considers the data and measurements we want to collect at the beginning of our campaigns.
    a. Highly agree (5)
    b. Somewhat agree (3)
    c. Not sure (0)
    d. Somewhat disagree (0)
    e. Highly disagree (0)
26. Each campaign has well-defined, measurable goals.
    a. Highly agree (5)
    b. Somewhat agree (3)
    c. Not sure (0)
    d. Somewhat disagree (0)
    e. Highly disagree (0)
27. Our marketing team develops personas.
    a. Highly agree (5)
    b. Somewhat agree (3)
    c. Not sure (0)
    d. Somewhat disagree (0)
    e. Highly disagree (0)
28. Personas are developed based on profile data from existing customers.
    a. Highly agree (5)
    b. Somewhat agree (3)
    c. Not sure (0)

    d. Somewhat disagree (0)

    e. Highly disagree (0)

29. Marketing has developed a content map that aligns to our personas and customer funnel stages.

    a. Highly agree (5)

    b. Somewhat agree (3)

    c. Not sure (0)

    d. Somewhat disagree (0)

    e. Highly disagree (0)

30. Our marketing team reviews and updates our content map at least once per year.

    a. Highly agree (5)

    b. Somewhat agree (3)

    c. Not sure (0)

    d. Somewhat disagree (0)

    e. Highly disagree (0)

31. Our content marketing team uses the content map to plan content creation.

    a. Highly agree (5)

    b. Somewhat agree (3)

    c. Not sure (0)

    d. Somewhat disagree (0)

    e. Highly disagree (0)

32. Each piece of content created has a measurable, quantifiable goal.

    a. Highly agree (5)

    b. Somewhat agree (3)

    c. Not sure (0)

    d. Somewhat disagree (0)

    e. Highly disagree (0)

33. The marketing team works collaboratively to manage across channels and platforms.

    a. Highly agree (5)

    b. Somewhat agree (3)

    c. Not sure (0)

    d. Somewhat disagree (0)

    e. Highly disagree (0)

34. The current martech stack we have in place meets or exceeds all of our marketing data tracking and reporting needs.

    a. Highly agree (5)

    b. Somewhat agree (3)

    c. Not sure (0)

    d. Somewhat disagree (0)

    e. Highly disagree (0)

35. I feel confident that the current martech stack is providing accurate reporting and data.

    a. Highly agree (5)

    b. Somewhat agree (3)

    c. Not sure (0)

    d. Somewhat disagree (0)

    e. Highly disagree (0)

36. We regularly perform A|B or multivariate tests across our marketing tactics.

    a. Highly agree (5)

    b. Somewhat agree (3)

    c. Not sure (0)

    d. Somewhat disagree (0)

    e. Highly disagree (0)

37. We have an established attribution model.

    a. Highly agree (5)

    b. Somewhat agree (3)

    c. Not sure (0)

    d. Somewhat disagree (0)

    e. Highly disagree (0)

38. The attribution model we currently use is: (Select all that apply.)

    a. First touch (2)

    b. Last touch (2)

    c. We use a multi-touch model. (5)

    d. We do not currently have an attribution model. (0)

39. We use default reporting from channels and platforms for our primary reporting.
    a. Highly agree (0)
    b. Somewhat agree (0)
    c. Not sure (0)
    d. Somewhat disagree (3)
    e. Highly disagree (5)
40. Marketing has defined, quantifiable KPIs.
    a. Highly agree (5)
    b. Somewhat agree (3)
    c. Not sure (0)
    d. Somewhat disagree (0)
    e. Highly disagree (0)

5. EMBRACING DATA-FIRST

41. The CMO has a close, strategic relationship with the CEO.
    a. Highly agree (5)
    b. Somewhat agree (3)
    c. Not sure (0)
    d. Somewhat disagree (0)
    e. Highly disagree (0)
42. The CMO has a close, strategic relationship with the CFO.
    a. Highly agree (5)
    b. Somewhat agree (3)
    c. Not sure (0)
    d. Somewhat disagree (0)
    e. Highly disagree (0)
43. The CMO has a close, strategic relationship with sales leadership.
    a. Highly agree (5)
    b. Somewhat agree (3)
    c. Not sure (0)
    d. Somewhat disagree (0)
    e. Highly disagree (0)

44. The CMO has a close, strategic relationship with the CIO and/or the IT department.
    a. Highly agree (5)
    b. Somewhat agree (3)
    c. Not sure (0)
    d. Somewhat disagree (0)
    e. Highly disagree (0)
45. The marketing team exhibits a growth mindset.
    a. Highly agree (5)
    b. Somewhat agree (3)
    c. Not sure (0)
    d. Somewhat disagree (0)
    e. Highly disagree (0)
46. The marketing staff has strong critical thinking skills.
    a. Highly agree (5)
    b. Somewhat agree (3)
    c. Not sure (0)
    d. Somewhat disagree (0)
    e. Highly disagree (0)
47. The marketing department documents and follows an established process.
    a. Highly agree (5)
    b. Somewhat agree (3)
    c. Not sure (0)
    d. Somewhat disagree (0)
    e. Highly disagree (0)
48. Marketing and organizational goals are part of each employee's reviews.
    a. Highly agree (5)
    b. Somewhat agree (3)
    c. Not sure (0)
    d. Somewhat disagree (0)
    e. Highly disagree (0)

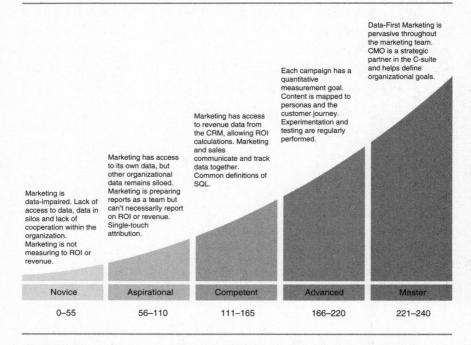

Marketing is data-impaired. Lack of access to data, data in silos and lack of cooperation within the organization. Marketing is not measuring to ROI or revenue.

Marketing has access to its own data, but other organizational data remains siloed. Marketing is preparing reports as a team but can't necessarily report on ROI or revenue. Single-touch attribution.

Marketing has access to revenue data from the CRM, allowing ROI calculations. Marketing and sales communicate and track data together. Common definitions of SQL.

Each campaign has a quantitative measurement goal. Content is mapped to personas and the customer journey. Experimentation and testing are regularly performed.

Data-First Marketing is pervasive throughout the marketing team. CMO is a strategic partner in the C-suite and helps define organizational goals.

Novice	Aspirational	Competent	Advanced	Master
0–55	56–110	111–165	166–220	221–240

FIGURE 4.2   The Data-First Marketing Maturity Model with Score Ranges.

Now, total up your score. The score for each answer appears in parentheses after the answer you select.

How did you do? Let's compare your total score with the ranges on the maturity model, referring to Figure 4.2 for reference.

0–55: Novice Stage

If your organization scored in the Novice Stage, you have a difficult time starting out with data-first marketing because these types of organizations often lack access to the data they need, or that data may be stored in silos throughout the organization. This makes it nearly impossible to measure ROI or revenue impact because the foundational data is not there to measure.

At this stage, organizations are not yet ready to access their own data for analysis, let alone leverage it. Processes, data and technology architecture, and other areas most likely need an overhaul before analysis can take place. Organizations in the Novice Stage mainly utilize out-of-the-box reporting from individual martech platforms and have limited or no sales and marketing integration and reporting.

Where does one begin? The following chapters of this book will walk you through every step you need to get on the right path to begin tracking data and sharing data across the organization as well as how to think about your martech planning and marketing analysis as you progress in the Data-First Marketing Maturity Model.

56–110: Aspirational Stage

If your organization scored in the Aspirational Stage, you've begun your data-first journey, but there is still a way to go. These organizations may have adopted a single-touch attribution model and have access to their own marketing data for analysis. Yet they still often lack access to data across the organization, such as revenue data from the sales team and the CRM and are only loosely aligned with the sales team. The intent is there, but the data is not complete.

Return to the assessment. It is organized into the five segments that align with the next five chapters. In which segments did you score lowest? While all five steps will be helpful to review, particularly focus on the chapter that corresponds to the areas where your organization appears to need the most growth to achieve data-first marketing maturity.

111–165: Competent Stage

If your organization scored in the Competent Stage, you're well on your way to success. Here again, there is substantial room for growth. Organizations in this stage likely have access to revenue data and are calculating marketing ROI. They are likely to have a strong alignment with sales around the marketing and sales funnel and the definition of a sales qualified lead (SQL). This alignment is further reflected by closer integration of marketing tools, such as marketing automation and sales CRM, enabling ROI and goals-based reporting with at least some multi-touch attribution.

Which areas does the organization in the Competent Stage need to focus on to achieve data-first marketing? Again, return to the assessment. It is organized into the five segments that align with the next five chapters. In which segments did you score lowest? While all five steps will be helpful to review, particularly focus on the chapter that corresponds to the areas where your organization can achieve the most growth along the path to data-first marketing maturity.

166–220: Advanced Stage

If your organization scored in the Advanced Stage, you've nearly mastered data-first principles. Your organization is fully aligned with sales, from processes to data integration. With this alignment, marketing is able to build strong buyer personas based on actual customer data and create content and targeting for campaigns based on this customer data. The marketing organization has access to a unified data view and is capable of customizable analysis and visualization. Marketing operations data is regularly analyzed and used to improve campaign and program performance and efficiency by some but not all the marketing team.

Which areas does the organization in the Advanced Stage need to focus on to achieve data-first marketing? Again, return to the assessment. The five segments align with the next five chapters of the book. In which segments did you score lowest? While all five steps will be helpful to review, particularly focus on the chapter that corresponds to the areas where your organization appears to need the most growth to achieve data-first marketing mastery.

221–240: Master Stage

Organizations scoring above 220 fall into the Master Stage of the Data-First Marketing Maturity Model. These are organizations who have all the aspects of data-first marketing transformation: people, process, technology, data, and especially culture. Insights from marketing data analytics are used in day-to-day marketing activities by the entire marketing team. Marketing is aligned with the business and recognized as a driver of rapid innovation and growth.

Not all organizations will achieve the Master Stage; we expect most organizations who undergo this transformation to aim for Advanced but more likely will remain in Competent with some aspects of Advanced.

If you look closely at the different stages, you will see that the size of your company (and your marketing budget) is not a factor in the stage you can achieve. Yes, large companies can afford to hire data scientists, but as we saw in the Gartner 2018 Marketing Analytics Survey, 45% of marketing organizations had these expensive resources doing basic tasks, most notably cleaning up the data, and that's even assuming they had the right data to begin with. Translated, this means that these organizations never completed the Aspirational Stage or the Competent Stage before trying to get right to analysis that they were not prepared for. While large companies can afford a CDP (customer data platform) to get to a unified data view and the resources to help them get it right, their requirements are very likely much more complex and involved than a smaller company. On the other hand, large companies most likely have spent the time and resources to define goals and strategies, whereas smaller companies might be more in reactive or survival mode where the only "strategy" is getting revenue in the door.

Regardless of what stage you find yourself in, don't be discouraged by where you are today; what matters is that you begin to change. Remember this adage: How do you eat an elephant? One bite at a time. Now let's get started!

CHAPTER 5

Step 1: Marketing-Business Alignment

First and foremost, achieving data-first marketing requires aligning marketing's strategy, goals, and objectives with those of the business. All too often, however, the CMO may not be involved in setting these organizational goals. In part this may stem from a marginalization of the marketing team as merely a cost center rather than a revenue-generating arm of the company. To rectify this situation requires relationship-building with the key stakeholders in the company, including the CEO, and the sales, finance, and IT leadership.

In this chapter we'll address the first step in the data-first marketing process: aligning the marketing team with strategic business teams and partners. These partnerships will not only help us to understand the goals of the business but also strengthen marketing's voice and help provide access to the data we need to evaluate marketing performance against business goals.

IS MARKETING A COST CENTER OR A REVENUE CENTER?

What is the perception of marketing in your company? If you polled your company today, would the CEO and other C-suite executives perceive marketing as a cost center or a revenue center? A cost center is a department often viewed as a necessary business expense – but it remains an expense – whereas a revenue center is perceived as a department that generates business income. For many organizations, there exist only tenuous ties between strategy, performance metrics,

67

and justifying marketing budgets to the financial stakeholders, often the CFO and CEO. From the CFO's perspective, marketing is a cost center rather than a revenue center. The 2018 Bizible State of Pipeline report found that more than half of marketers believe that the marketing organization is perceived as a cost center rather than a revenue center by the organization.

In a 2016 study by *Chief Marketer*, over 50% of C-suite executives didn't think that the company's marketing expenditure was significantly driving top-line revenue or even profits. That's a real problem for the marketing team when trying to convince the organization to justify or increase marketing budgets.

Further, being perceived as a cost center rather than a revenue center puts the bullseye on the team's back when downsizing occurs. As J.T. O'Donnell, founder and CEO of WorkItDaily.com and a former HR executive warned in an article for *Inc.* magazine, "in a time of economic crisis, companies focus on keeping employees with the greatest return on investment (ROI)."

So how can marketing change this dynamic and become perceived as a revenue center? It begins with demonstrating value to the CEO and the C-suite – specifically using data to show how marketing campaigns and activities increase company value and revenue.

SHIFTING THE PERCEPTION OF MARKETING FROM COST CENTER TO REVENUE CENTER

Given that the main goal of the CEO and the business is to increase business value, mainly through revenue generation, what metrics can the marketing team provide that demonstrate success? Clearly revenue generated is the best metric, but what if the marketing team doesn't have access to that data? As with any goal, it helps to start with the goal and work backward to determine what steps (and in this case, metrics) help identify progress toward meeting that goal.

Measuring revenue generation may involve systems that are often not owned or managed by the marketing team as well, especially for companies that do not generate revenue through online methods. For many software as a service (SaaS) companies, however, ROI can likely be determined through tools the marketing team does own, like Google Analytics. Using Google Analytics' ecommerce goal tracking, companies can directly view revenue generation and attribute it to specific campaigns and marketing channels.

In contrast, offline revenue generation companies face a greater challenge of combining data from various systems to achieve true campaign ROI metrics. As marketers look to glean data from these systems, we first must understand which metrics we're looking for from these systems. Marketers likely have quantitative data in marketing systems, but you may not have all of the data you need, depending on the business goal you're trying to measure. Additionally, some metrics also require the sales team or other departments to keep data current in their system. For example, if a salesperson does not update the opportunity's revenue, reports on revenue potential will be inaccurate.

By forging relationships with key stakeholders, the CMO and the marketing team can begin to establish trust and support from the other areas of the organization. Through these partnerships, marketing can gain access to the data it needs to report on the most important metrics, including revenue, for the organization and thereby building marketing's reputation and value as revenue center rather than a cost center.

GETTING BUY-IN FROM KEY STAKEHOLDERS

The beautiful thing about data is that it can create a common language between multiple business groups once we agree on the data and measurement that is important. "As data and analytics become pervasive, the ability to communicate in this language, to becoming data literate, is the new organizational readiness factor," said Gartner Senior Director Analyst Carlie Idoine. "If there is no common language with which to interpret the various data sources in the organization, there will be fundamental communication challenges when using data- and analytics-based solutions." Regardless of the stakeholder you may be addressing, sharing a common data measurement and goals is key to organizational success, including for marketing.

But we also must be careful of inundating our stakeholders with a deluge of data. Examining every data point will lead to data exhaustion and distraction. Each stakeholder has organizational priorities that we must address.

CEO

Each role in an organization has its own responsibilities, and the CEO position is no different. Using a sports analogy, CEOs are the coaches and general managers of the team. If the coach or general manager doesn't meet the team's goals, they are fired. The same is typically true for the CEO.

Wikipedia defines the CEO as being "charged with maximizing the value of the entity, which may include maximizing the share price, market share, revenues or another element." Many CEOs were hired by and report to a board of directors. When the board meets quarterly to review the CEO's performance during that past quarter, they are essentially measuring how the company performed during that period. And the buck stops with the CEO.

Even if a company doesn't have a board of directors or isn't publicly traded, CEOs still have a core responsibility to maximize the company's value through revenue. Simple profit and loss principles dictate that if the company does not make enough revenue then cuts must be made to expenses – in costs across the board – including marketing budgets and staff. Ultimately, your CEO cares about increasing the company's value – bringing value to the shareholders and keeping the company viable.

Because of this focus, the CEO has specific success metrics for the organization, not the least of which is revenue generation and stock price. To review, while ROI and revenue reporting is ideal, 85% of CEOs want marketers to at minimum report on:

1. Lead volume (SQLs)
2. Lead to opportunity rate
3. Cost per qualified lead acquisition
4. Opportunity revenue potential (i.e., sales pipeline)
5. Revenue generated

While there are KPIs and measurements we may use inside of the marketing team to judge our own progress toward ROI, revenue and these five CEO goals, ultimately our reporting to the CEO should focus primarily on metrics that best demonstrate marketing's progression toward increased revenue and ROI.

CEOs are ready to believe in marketing and welcome marketing into overall business objective and goal setting. A 2019 McKinsey and Company study reported that 83% of CEOs are eager to have marketing become a major driver of growth. To get the CEO in your corner, however, marketing must prove how it is driving growth. With the right data and measurement, marketing can prove this value to the CEO and the organization, but it takes a larger transformation and partnership across the entire C-suite.

Sales Leadership

Similar to the CEO, sales leadership will ultimately be measured by revenue generation. In most cases, the sales team is financially incentivized through sales commissions to focus primarily on revenue generation. But sales leadership can't accomplish the team's goals without support from marketing. Unfortunately, as Figure 5.1 shows, while the sales team often views marketing as "creative" and "flexible," marketing isn't always viewed as "results-driven."

Just about any study you read will confirm that organizations that achieve a high level of marketing and sales alignment realize greater revenue than those that do not achieve this alignment. LinkedIn's research shows that businesses with strong sales and marketing alignment are 67% more effective at closing deals, 58% more effective at retaining customers, and drive 208% more revenue as a result of their marketing efforts.

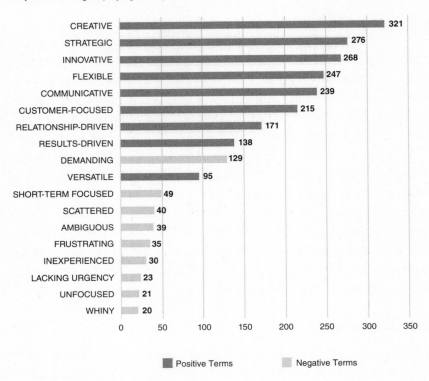

Sales Views Marketing As ...

Below displays sales' sentiments toward their marketing counterparts with a weighted response ranking displaying the top five terms selected, with higher ratings for top selections

FIGURE 5.1   How Sales Perceives Marketing.

Source: The LeadMD Sales and Marketing Alignment Survey Benchmarking & Insights Report © 2019 LeadMD & Drift.

While each of the company stakeholders plays a role in how marketing is perceived and the involvement marketing may have in the development of the company's strategy, goals, and objectives, perhaps none is more important and immediate than marketing's relationship with sales. Changing sales' perception of marketing and proving the value of marketing efforts depends on marketing's quantitative measurement of meeting sales' goals. First, marketing must truly achieve alignment with sales.

But what does sales and marketing alignment really mean? Like many things, including data-first marketing, there is a spectrum of alignment along which companies fall. At one end is limited alignment where sales and marketing are siloed organizations; they don't talk to each other or have shared goals. Perhaps marketing even produces content and campaigns in a vacuum of actual sales needs and usage.

Their data and reporting are most likely separate, which means that end-to-end reporting, from lead acquisition to customer revenue, is not possible.

According to the 2017 Business Performance Benchmark Study from Altify, while the majority of marketing and sales organizations report that the two work well together, only 54% of salespeople agreed that "marketing in our company is an effective investment of the company's resources." Marketing staff was much more optimistic, with 86% agreeing with the same statement. So, what's causing the disconnect between sales and marketing?

Televerde (2017) surveyed more than 200 sales leaders in their "What Does Sales Need and Want from Marketing?" study. The top three reasons that sales gave for this misalignment were:

1. Lack of regular communication (37%)
2. The lead qualification process (30%)
3. Differences in the way sales and marketing successes are measured (33%)

1. Regular Communication

If we're truly going to treat sales like a partner and seek their guidance and support, we have to regularly communicate with sales to solve problems and report on results. To solve that lack of regular communication, have a regular meeting with sales leadership to discuss results, get feedback, and actively involve sales in the marketing strategy discussion.

Account-based marketing (ABM) has become a hugely hot focus area in marketing over the last few years and represents a key opportunity for close communication and strategy with the sales team. ABM is a marketing strategy that directs marketing resources to engage a specific set of target accounts. But who develops this list of accounts to target?

In my many conversations with marketing teams over the years, we'd often introduce ABM as a possible strategy for ensuring that a company's brand and personalized message appeared to the right audiences – audiences in companies being actively targeted by the sales team for new accounts. However, in most cases, the marketing team had not worked jointly with the sales team to identify the target accounts. While account-based marketing is a great buzzword, marketers are not always executing ABM in tandem with sales. In a 2018 study on account-based marketing by Ascend2, marketers shared that targeting ideal accounts is both a top priority and a top challenge (see Figure 5.2).

And while a conversation with the sales team about which accounts to target is helpful, it remains qualitative, anecdotal data versus quantitative data. ABM is just one example of how marketing

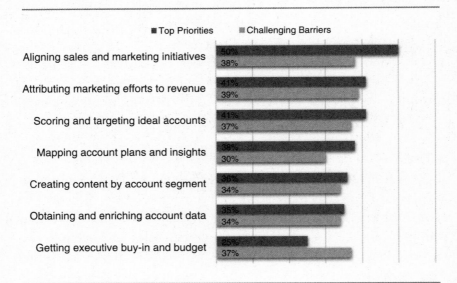

FIGURE 5.2   Top Priorities and Biggest Challenges of Account-Based Marketing.

Source: "Account-Based Marketing Strategy Survey" by Ascend2 and Research Partners, January 2018.

can lead the conversation with the sales team using quantitative customer data and steer the agreement on the target account list. The LeadMD/Drift study showed that qualitative data from sales and marketing may not always accurately represent success. The study further found that those who experience more successful outcomes also were more likely to conduct their account targeting jointly, as compared to marketers who lead that planning with some sales involvement (see Figure 5.3).

But this communication effort must also work both ways. Here's a true story from our past as an example. One hour before a response to a major RFP was due, a salesperson requested marketing help. The marketing team created a customized product sheet just in time for the deadline. Was this an example of good sales and marketing alignment? On one hand, sales needed specific content created to win a deal and the marketing team immediately delivered. On the other hand, marketing wasn't given ample response time or included in the RFP preparation process.

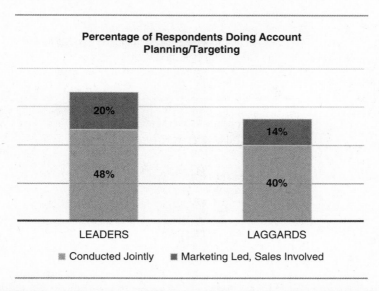

FIGURE 5.3   Percentage of Marketers Who Jointly Plan and Target Accounts with the Sales Team.

Source: The LeadMD Sales and Marketing Alignment Survey Benchmarking & Insights Report © 2019 LeadMD & Drift.

In creating an open line of communication with the sales team, it's also incumbent on the marketing leadership to push back on the sales team and insist on involvement in the sales process. Marketing efforts, as our RFP story illustrates, do not stop with a handoff to sales. Rather, marketing and sales need to communicate and work seamlessly to qualify leads and drive them to become customers.

2. Lead Qualification

Lead qualification requires a common definition with the sales team. Instead of defining your funnel stages and definitions in a vacuum, work with sales to define the MAL, MQL, SAL, and SQL. Define what the handoff from sales should entail – when should a lead move from MQL to SAL status? Sales should help define what types of leads they need with you. Figure 5.4 demonstrates a sample marketing and

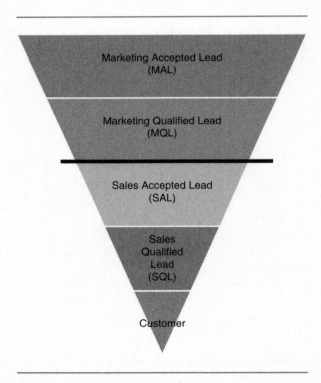

FIGURE 5.4   Sample Lead Qualification Funnel.

sales funnel that your team may adopt, with the bold black line representing the lead handoff from marketing to sales.

The aforementioned study by LeadMD/Drift published research findings around sales and marketing alignment. From their research, they developed a measurement for ascertaining how well sales and marketing were working together toward two common goals: performance (growth in revenue, wins, and lead quality over a three-year period) and pipeline (growth and sustainability in predictable revenue). The outcome was surprising. Self-reported marketing-sales alignment (qualitative) did not also reflect in performance growth (quantitative), as reflected in Figure 5.5, which shows

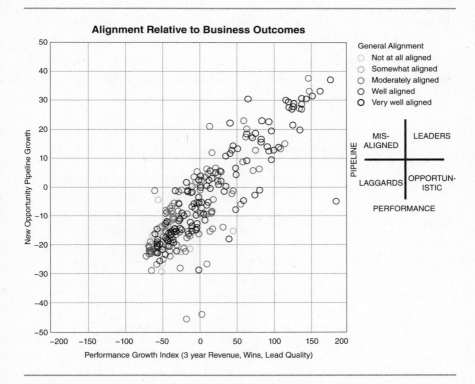

FIGURE 5.5   Alignment Relative to Business Outcomes.

Source: The LeadMD Sales and Marketing Alignment Survey Benchmarking & Insights Report © 2019 LeadMD & Drift.

how qualitatively reported sales and marketing alignment related to quantitative business outcomes.

Interestingly, while marketers would often consider a common definition with the sales team of the marketing and sales funnel as the core factor for organizational alignment, commonly defined and aligned KPIs between marketing and sales did not always reflect performance and pipeline success. In the LeadMD/Drift study, marketing and sales executives were not necessarily associating performance with their definition of alignment. Out of 70 factors, the executives ranked these five as the most important to sales and marketing alignment. Figure 5.6 shows the top five KPIs that sales and marketing executives deemed essential to sales and marketing alignment, and the correlation to how aligned they perceived their departments to be with one another.

While these five factors were most correlated to the executives' perception of alignment, lack of achievement around these very KPIs did not negatively influence that perception. As long as the sales and

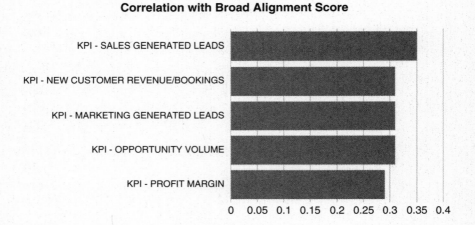

FIGURE 5.6   Correlation with Broad Alignment Score.

Source: The LeadMD Sales Marketing Alignment Survey Benchmarking & Insights Report © 2019 LeadMD & Drift.

marketing teams shared the KPI, alignment was perceived between the two organizations, even if it did not equate to successful outcomes.

What this study proves is that marketing can't truly be aligned with sales just by creating common definitions of stages of the funnel and the qualification definition for each stage. Rather, it also requires *measurement* to understand if those commonly defined stages and KPIs are successful and how we can continue to improve to meet business goals together.

3. Sales and Marketing Measurement

To align sales and marketing measurement, the marketing team also needs access to customer data to gauge how the two teams are working together to reach their common goals for each stage of the funnel. The LeadMD/Drift study indicated that a shared tech stack facilitates the visibility and togetherness that leads to success. And those in the study that were considered laggards reported significantly more disjointed technology when it came to measuring lead routing, with lead progression data often owned solely by sales with no marketing input. This is a common issue we've seen with our own marketing clients over the years. Without access to critical lead progression data through the funnel and ultimately sales outcome data in the form of closed deals and revenue, marketing's reporting can be severely limited.

As you measure lead progression, know too that marketing's efforts may not be the reason that a lead does not progress further in the sales funnel. While sales may work with the marketing team to develop content to help develop and close opportunities, the sales team doesn't always work with the marketing team to develop the sales process or scripts. Having lead information pass between both the sales and marketing teams allows marketing to evaluate how the sales leads are being processed.

For example, we had a client who uses Marketo for their marketing automation software and Salesforce as their CRM. While Marketo is mainly owned by the marketing team and is considered a marketing tool and Salesforce is owned by the sales team and is mainly considered a sales tool, information from each tool syncs with the other, allowing the marketing team clear visibility into how leads are processed once they have been handed to the sales team. As we might expect, the sales team always yearns for higher-quality leads – leads that more closely resemble a customer or represent a hot prospect. Higher-quality leads likely mean a faster path to a sale, and thus a faster path to sales commission.

In the case of our customer, we utilized LinkedIn Ads to target very specific professional demographics requested by the sales team. By the looks of the conversions being generated from the ads, it appeared that the campaign was working well at driving leads with specific professional demographic qualifications. However, sales continued to report a low lead-to-opportunity ratio, meaning that leads were not becoming opportunities and leading sales to question the true quality of the leads that marketing was generating from the campaign.

We took a deeper look into a handful of specific leads that initially appeared to have the right target professional demographics, such as titles, experience, and company names that would signify that lead as a marketing-qualified lead and initiate a lead handoff to the sales team. As we began to dig into the leads, we saw what may have been the issue. While the leads appeared to be high quality, the sales process may not have been working as intended. The sales process involved emailing the lead, but in many cases the process never involved making a direct phone call to the lead.

The challenge with relying on emailing a lead is that you aren't always aware if the lead actually received and read your email or if the email was marked as spam. While marketing automation tools, like Marketo, give marketers testing features to try to prevent an email from being marked as spam by the recipient's server, CRMs like Salesforce and email software like Microsoft Outlook typically do not have these testing features. Further, while open rate as a measurement isn't always exact, it can help marketers to identify if the email was received and avoided the spam folder; again, however, sales teams often do not have these tools at their disposal.

Evaluating the emails being sent revealed another possible issue: the email script.

My guess, John, is that we're out of touch for one of three reasons:

1. I have done something to offend you.
2. You are working with someone else and just don't want to hurt my feelings by telling me.
3. You want desperately to call me back, but are trapped under something heavy, and cannot reach your keyboard.

I'd consider it a personal favor if you'd let me know if the problem is one of these, or something I didn't think of. If it's #3, reply to this email and I'll send help!

Best,
Joe

Unfortunately, sales emails like this are quite common. But are they really effective? Are they designed to make the prospect laugh and incentivize them to respond? It's hard to know exactly why sales takes this approach. Still other salespeople try to connect with prospects by cyberstalking them, like this email we received to consider changing our 401(k) provider:

Janet,
I noticed we don't have much for common connections to get a warm intro, so I hope it's alright I'm reaching out directly.

I noticed you're leading a growing team at Marketing Mojo, and thought you'd want to know how we're helping scaling companies offer 401(k) plans while managing their IRS compliance, all at an affordable cost.

As fiduciaries, we have a responsibility to make sure your employees are paying the lowest cost fees for their plan, which in turn:

(continued)

(*Continued*)

- Reduces your liability
- Prevents you from failing nondiscrimination testing by proactively testing your plan
- Maximizes employee deductions by actively monitoring plans performance

If you're the right person to talk to about setting up Marketing Mojo's benefits, what does your calendar look like? If not, who do you suggest I reach out to instead?

Thanks,
Bob

Nice try, Bob, but you missed the mark. Now we just think you're stalking us.

When you see potential issues like this, it presents an opportunity for marketing to work more deeply with sales to help craft and define messaging and, more importantly, measure its effectiveness!

As our examples show, unencumbered access to necessary data by both marketing and sales is necessary to understand and measure success in the teams' combined goals. Further, however, if the data between the two organizations isn't clean and integrated, it will be difficult to quantify value. A 2017 study from Allocadia found that nearly 50% of marketing and sales data was either messy or in the process of being reformatted for reporting, as shown in Figure 5.7.

In the partnership with sales, marketing must help define established data policies between the marketing and sales organizations. Without established processes and rules about how data is entered and standards for nomenclature and data entry, data can quickly become muddled and useless to either party.

At one company, Julia's marketing team inherited a Salesforce database that had a lot of old, irrelevant data. There were thousands of leads that listed no originating lead source. Were they generated from trade shows? Were they generated from organic search? Without a lead source and without knowing if these contacts had opted in to

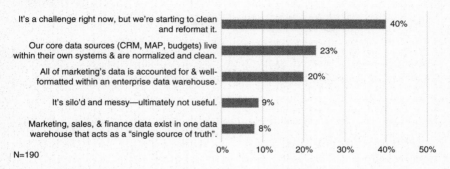

How would you rate the overall state of your company's Marketing and Sales data?

- It's a challenge right now, but we're starting to clean and reformat it. — **40%**
- Our core data sources (CRM, MAP, budgets) live within their own systems & are normalized and clean. — **23%**
- All of marketing's data is accounted for & well-formatted within an enterprise data warehouse. — **20%**
- It's silo'd and messy—ultimately not useful. — **9%**
- Marketing, sales, & finance data exist in one data warehouse that acts as a "single source of truth". — **8%**

N=190

FIGURE 5.7   How Marketers Rate the Overall State of the Company's Marketing and Sales Data.

Source: From Allocadia 2017 Marketing Performance Management Maturity Study

receive emails, her team could not use them for outbound campaigns from the marketing automation platform Marketo. The marketing team spent substantial time cleaning up the database and then, just as importantly, setting up new data policies for both marketing and sales coupled with customizations for Salesforce and Marketo to match. By considering the metrics the marketing team would need for revenue and pipeline reporting down the road, the team defined the process for sales to enter specific information in Salesforce as they updated their opportunities.

Establishing data policies, however, does little good if there is not agreement and training by both groups. Julia's marketing team held a meeting with the sales team, training them on how to follow the new data policies. The marketing team's leadership on data policy established company data governance policies and sales-marketing processes defined with integrated data repositories. It enabled the marketing team to generate end-to-end reporting and demonstrate campaign influence on pipeline and revenue.

Having a policy alone, however, does not ensure marketing or sales staff will follow those policies. Data policies also require an established method of measurement and enforcement to ensure compliance. One of the best methods to ensure sales compliance with data policies is to tie sales compensation to data policy fulfillment.

At ScienceLogic, Julia encountered a true data-first sales leader. When the new senior vice president of sales (SVP) started at the company, he brought with him much of his extended sales team, including a dedicated sales operations (sales ops) team member, who acquired management of the Salesforce CRM system from marketing. Once data policies were established, the sales ops team member heavily customized the Salesforce CRM with metrics and reporting to track sales pipeline and opportunities in the way that the SVP needed to visualize and manage them. He also held mandatory sales meetings each week, and each salesperson was required to update their data in Salesforce prior to that meeting because they would be held accountable for the data provided. Marketing was included in the weekly sales calls, strengthening marketing's understanding of lead status and strengthening sales and marketing alignment.

Further strengthening the sales and marketing relationship, the SVP strongly supported the marketing team and its efforts. When marketing needed all contacts associated with a opportunity linked to that sale, he supported the effort and required the sales team to make these updates, even tying compensation to it, helping marketing to track the multiple marketing touches that lead to a sale.

What this sales leader understood was the importance of data – not just to marketing but to the entire organization and its success. He embraced transparency and enforced data integrity throughout the sales organization. Tying the data to compensation helped ensure that the data was both accurate and complete. His processes broke down salesperson-specific silos of data and ensured that important customer data belonged to and was shared across the company, to achieve company goals and not just individual ones.

Work with sales leadership to understand the process for the sales team to update data. Good sales leadership will generally place a high level of importance on keeping lead, opportunity, and pipeline data current. And also ensure that the sales team utilizes common definitions and practices so that marketing can understand data and challenges.

Finance Leadership

According to Bizible's 2018 State of Pipeline report, marketers who reported ROI of 1.5x or greater were 111% more likely to be perceived as a revenue center in their organizations. All too often marketing is perceived as an overhead expense, leaving marketing vulnerable to cuts. In the aforementioned 2019 McKinsey and Company study, 45% of CFOs surveyed said the reason marketing proposals have been declined or not fully funded in the past is because they didn't demonstrate a clear line to value. Marketing needs to prove its value to CFOs to ensure proper funding and to be respected as a strategic partner.

A perception transformation from cost center to revenue center also gives marketing a power boost. CFOs are also taking on more strategic roles in organizations, according to a 2016 survey by Intacct. By transforming marketing from cost center to strategic partner and revenue center, the marketing team will have more influence and input into the overall strategic direction of the company.

However, perceptions aren't going to change unless marketing establishes a better relationship with finance and provides measurable financial impact for the organization. Many marketing teams still do not have a close relationship with finance, with more marketers responding, "We speak only when forced to," than marketers responding that finance is a strategic partner. (see Figure 5.8).

To begin, marketing must speak the language of finance. As Debbie Qaqish, chief strategy officer of the Pedowitz Group, surmises, "The CFO and the CMO speak two different languages if marketing is not a revenue marketing organization. The CFO speaks the language of business: cost, revenue, bookings, and forecasts. A traditional marketer is speaking the language of creative impressions and traffic. No one, especially the C-Suite, cares about the colors of

How would you describe Marketing's relationship with Finance?

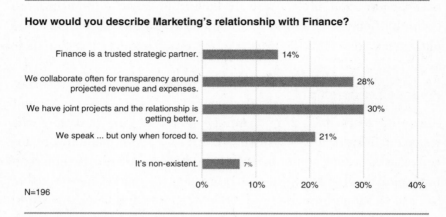

N=196

FIGURE 5.8   How Marketers Rate Their Relationship with Finance.
Source: From Allocadia 2017 Marketing Performance Management Maturity Study

the website. When a marketing organization is focused on revenue marketing, you will find the CMO and the CFO speaking the same language."

Make the CFO and finance leadership a strategic partner in setting your budgets and marketing goals. Come prepared to meetings with finance with quantitative revenue performance data as well as revenue projections based on historical performance.

IT Leadership

The relationship between the CIO and CMO is becoming increasingly important. Given the complexity of the martech stack today, marketing must have a symbiotic relationship with IT. Marketers aren't necessarily experts in how systems integrate, and there are times when marketing needs greater technical assistance to integrate data across disparate platforms. The CIO and IT help lead that charge with their expertise. In fact, according to the IDG 2020 State of the CIO survey, CIOs report that they're increasingly assisting marketing with determining and defining business needs, researching products and vendors, and helping with data analysis.

And just like CMOs, CIOs are feeling an increased obligation to tie their efforts to business outcomes. In IDG's 2019 report, 81% of CIOs responded that they are under extreme pressure to defend their investments and prove ROI.

One of the more frequent pitfalls we find that marketers experience with IT is related to the project queue. The IT department continues to have increased demand from various departments, leading to a backlog of projects. All too often, we've seen marketing teams have a technical programming request to improve page load time on the website, a known Google ranking factor for SEO, only to see that request sit for months because of other projects that were prioritized in IT's queue.

Knowing that the CIO is likely prioritizing projects based on revenue impact and that the CIO also likely shares management of and analysis from the martech stack data, approach the CIO with your common interests. If the IT department can assist with integrating systems to access the data marketing needs to quantitatively measure revenue and ROI, the CIO should be compelled to prioritize marketing's IT requests.

GET STARTED TODAY

Marketing must regain a driving role in the direction of its budget, the business, and revenue generation. But that begins by making some fundamental shifts in how marketing is perceived in the organization. There's an opportunity at hand for marketers to lead organizational change and realize revenue success. It begins with three main steps.

1. Understand and Embrace the Business Goals

Before you can provide metrics that demonstrate marketing's contribution to revenue, you must first know the revenue goals and other primary objectives for the organization. In a perfect world, the marketing team has a role in the setting of these goals, but in most cases they do not. Whatever the goal is, discover it and determine how marketing efforts fit into realistically achieving that goal.

2. Rekindle the Marketing and Sales Relationship

Without a symbiotic relationship between marketing and sales, the marketing team may not have access to critical sales and revenue attribution information needed for revenue center-level reporting. Renew your relationship with the sales team and determine how to attain the information closest to revenue as possible, whether that data is limited to opportunities, sales qualified leads, or pipeline.

3. Establish a Reporting Plan for Key Metrics and Lead the Marketing Team

Once aligned with sales, establish a reporting plan with key metrics from both sales and marketing to demonstrate marketing's contribution to the revenue goals. Keep the sales team involved in your reporting to achieve understanding, transparency, and support as you both work together toward common revenue objectives. Work with sales to establish a data policy and metrics and develop ways to ensure data policy compliance.

CHAPTER 6

Step 2: Data Integration, Architecture and Technical Resources

Achieving the connection between business goals and marketing strategy and goals requires integration of data to measure success. But where do you get started? And how do you connect all of your disparate systems and data to ensure you're pulling the right data from the right sources to get the answers you need?

In this chapter we'll begin to evaluate the data you need, where it may reside, and who owns that data. Not all of the data will be integrated at the outset, so we'll cover ways to integrate the data to get a clearer picture of what the data is conveying. We'll address the importance of data governance and data policy to ensure a clean dataset, and finally, we'll cover how to create visualizations of the data to help convey the information more effectively.

DEVELOP A STRATEGY FOR YOUR MARTECH STACK

In order to really glean the data you need from the right sources to use for data-first marketing, you'll need to have a marketing technology (martech) stack in place. The martech stack is your group of technologies – platforms, software, and tools – that allow you to execute, manage, and measure your marketing efforts. It's likely to combine multiple items from Chiefmartec.com's Marketing Technology Landscape (see Figure 6.1), and it can seem overwhelming.

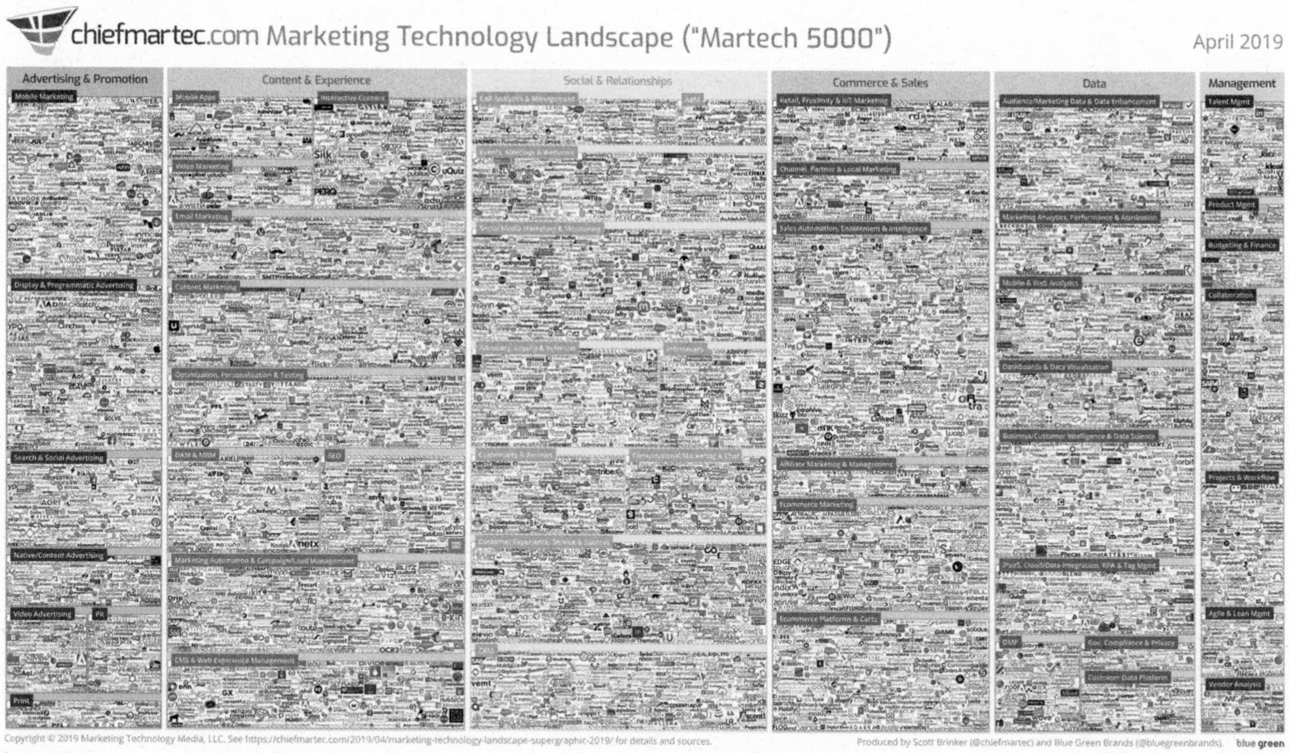

FIGURE 6.1 The 2019 Marketing Technology Landscape. Courtesy of Scott Brinker, chiefmartec.com

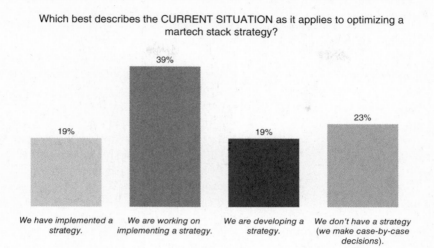

Which best describes the CURRENT SITUATION as it applies to optimizing a martech stack strategy?

FIGURE 6.2   Only 19% of marketers have actually implemented a martech stack strategy.

Source: Martech Stack Optimization, Ascend2

In many cases, marketers simply inherit various pieces of the martech stack from previous marketing teams. Martech can also be difficult and time-consuming to replace. In turn, many marketing organizations have not developed a clear plan for how the martech stack should be updated or grow. In the February 2020 Martech Stack Optimization study from Ascend2, only 19% of marketers reported having implemented a martech strategy, and a full 23% reported that they don't have a cohesive, common martech strategy at all (see Figure 6.2).

But your martech stack holds the key to the actionable information you need to achieve data-first marketing transformation. If your marketing organization doesn't yet have a martech stack strategy, you'll need to start by developing one. First, take an inventory of your current stack. What systems do you have in place? What data resides in each of these systems? For example, in our organization, our martech stack includes the following.

Data Source	Data It Holds
Accounting software	• Actual marketing spend • Actual revenue by client/project
Payroll software	• Personnel investments in the marketing department
Analytics software	• Traffic to the website • Origins of that traffic • Lead goals attained by that traffic
Google Ads	• Clicks from paid search ad campaigns • Conversions from paid search ad campaigns
LinkedIn Ads	• Clicks from LinkedIn Ads • Conversions from LinkedIn Ads
Marketing Automation software	• Marketing qualified leads • Campaign history by lead • Conversions from Google, LinkedIn Ads
CRM software	• Campaigns • Sales qualified leads • Opportunities with stages and values • Closed contract values and dates • Companies and contacts associated with closed contracts

SIX QUESTIONS TO ASK WHEN EVALUATING YOUR MARTECH STACK

Once you map out your current martech stack and where the data you need resides, you may find that you're missing certain pieces. When evaluating which pieces to add or which items should be replaced in the stack, there are six main questions to ask.

1. Do You Have the Data You Need to Show the Business Value of Marketing?

Mapping our current martech stack and what's needed for measurement can help identify the holes in the stack that may exist. Adding another column to the earlier mapping, we listed the items we want to measure along the path to measuring ROI.

Here's an example of our own martech stack mapping and how and which data sources hold the information we need to understand each business measurement.

Data I Need	Data Source(s)	Data It Holds
Traffic to the site by channel and/or campaign	Analytics software	• Traffic to the site by channel and/or campaign
Leads generated by channel and/or campaign	Analytics software Google Ads LinkedIn Ads Marketing automation software	• Goals set in analytics and channel/campaign • Conversions set in ad platforms and its campaign • Lead data/reporting by the date a lead was created and its channel/campaign
Lead conversion rate by channel and/or campaign	Analytics software Google Ads LinkedIn Ads Marketing automation software	• Goals set in analytics and channel/campaign along with traffic from those channels/campaigns • Conversions set in ad platforms and its campaign along with clicks to that campaign • Lead data/reporting by the date a lead was created and its channel/campaign, but may not have the traffic to the site for that channel/campaign
Marketing qualified leads by channel and/or campaign	Marketing automation software	• Leads that meet the MQL rules threshold by channel/campaign
MQL rate by channel and/or campaign	Marketing automation software	• Leads that meet the MQL rules threshold along with total leads generated by channel/campaign
Sales qualified leads by channel and/or campaign	Marketing automation software	• Leads that meet the SQL rules threshold by channel/campaign and were assigned to sales

(continued)

Data I Need	Data Source(s)	Data It Holds
SQL rate by channel and/or campaign	Marketing automation software	• Leads that meet the SQL rules threshold along with total leads generated by channel/campaign and were assigned to sales
Lead to opportunity rate by channel and/or campaign	Marketing automation software CRM software	• Total leads passed to sales (SQLs) by channel/campaign • Leads that became opportunities by channel/campaign
Opportunity to close won rate by channel and/or campaign	CRM software	• Total opportunities generated from marketing leads by channel/campaign • Total closed-won opportunities by channel/campaign
Average opportunity value by channel and/or campaign	CRM software	• Value of each opportunity generated my marketing by channel/campaign (take the average)
Total revenue generated by channel and/or campaign	CRM software accounting software	• Total of value of closed-won opportunities by channel/campaign
Lifetime value by channel and/or campaign	CRM software accounting software	• Closed-won opportunities by channel/campaign • Lifetime value of that contract to date
ROI by channel and/or campaign	Google Ads LinkedIn Ads CRM software accounting software	• Total of value of closed-won opportunities by channel/campaign • Total of marketing budget spent by channel/campaign • Possibly also include lifetime ROI with lifetime value of contract to date

While clearly important for measurement, pulling this data from disparate sources and then combining it to gain information can be time consuming.

2. Who Owns the Data Source and the Data within It?

As our mapping starts to unfold, we can begin to clearly identify where the data we need resides. Our mapping also begins to reveal data sources that are likely not owned by marketing, such as the accounting software. We must know who owns the data so that we can request data access from the group that holds that data. To clarify this, I've added another column (shown in gray) to my table to identify which department owns the data source:

Data I Need	Data Source(s)	Who Owns It	Data It Holds
Traffic to the site by channel and/or campaign	Analytics software	Marketing	• Traffic to the site by channel and/or campaign
Leads generated by channel and/or campaign	Analytics software Google Ads LinkedIn Ads Marketing automation software	Marketing Marketing Marketing Marketing	• Goals set in analytics and channel/campaign • Conversions set in ad platforms and its campaign • Lead data/reporting by the date a lead was created and its channel/campaign
Lead conversion rate by channel and/or campaign	Analytics software Google Ads LinkedIn Ads Marketing automation software	Marketing Marketing Marketing Marketing	• Goals set in analytics and channel/campaign along with traffic from those channels/campaigns • Conversions set in ad platforms and its campaign along with clicks to that campaign • Lead data/reporting by the date a lead was created and its channel/campaign, but may not have the traffic to the site for that channel/campaign

(continued)

Data I Need	Data Source(s)	Who Owns It	Data It Holds
Marketing qualified leads by channel and/or campaign	Marketing Automation software	Marketing	• Leads that meet the MQL rules threshold by channel/campaign
MQL rate by channel and/or campaign	Marketing automation software	Marketing	• Leads that meet the MQL rules threshold along with total leads generated by channel/campaign
Sales qualified leads by channel and/or campaign	Marketing automation software	Marketing	• Leads that meet the SQL rules threshold by channel/campaign and were assigned to sales
SQL rate by channel and/or campaign	Marketing automation software	Marketing	• Leads that meet the SQL rules threshold along with total leads generated by channel/campaign and were assigned to sales
Lead to opportunity rate by channel and/or campaign	Marketing automation software	Marketing	• Total leads passed to sales (SQLs) by channel/campaign
	CRM software	Sales	• Leads that became opportunities by channel/campaign
Opportunity to close won rate by channel and/or campaign	CRM software	Sales	• Total opportunities generated from marketing leads by channel/campaign • Total closed-won opportunities by channel/campaign
Average opportunity value by channel and/or campaign	CRM software	Sales	• Value of each opportunity generated my marketing by channel/campaign (take the average)

(*continued*)

Data I Need	Data Source(s)	Who Owns It	Data It Holds
Total revenue generated by channel and/or campaign	CRM software Accounting software	Sales Finance	• Total of value of closed-won opportunities by channel/campaign
Lifetime value by channel and/or campaign	CRM software accounting software	Sales Finance	• Closed-won opportunities by channel/campaign • Lifetime value of that contract to date
ROI by channel and/or campaign	Google Ads LinkedIn Ads CRM software accounting software	Marketing Marketing Sales Finance	• Total of value of closed-won opportunities by channel/campaign • Total of marketing budget spent by channel/campaign • Possibly also include lifetime ROI with lifetime value of contract to date

Data governance – the policies about how data is collected, stored, and shared within the organization – dictates who needs to grant marketing access to various data. Gartner defines data governance as "the specification of decision rights and an accountability framework to ensure the appropriate behavior in the valuation, creation, consumption and control of data and analytics." The owner of the data may not control the data policies, which may also mean that marketing must work with the controller of the data policies to ensure data governance compliance and ensure that new policies are created as needed to access this data.

3. What Level of Integration Do You Need to Run These Reports?

Accessing the data itself is only part of the issue. Can we integrate the data to see trends and glean insights from the data?

In the mapping above, for example, let's say we want to understand conversion rate from organic search. To calculate the conversion rate from a channel, we use this equation:

$$\frac{\text{Conversions by that channel}}{\text{Traffic from that channel}}$$

As the table shows, we can pull that data from one source, Analytics, because the analytics software provides us with both traffic by channel and conversions by channel. Additionally, in analytics software such as Google Analytics, the conversion rate may even be calculated directly in the platform for you.

However, with other measurements, you may need to combine data from multiple sources. This has been one of the greater challenges for marketers when addressing the features of their martech stack components. As shown in Figure 6.3, integration with other technologies in the stack continues to be a challenge for many marketers, according to the aforementioned Ascend2 study.

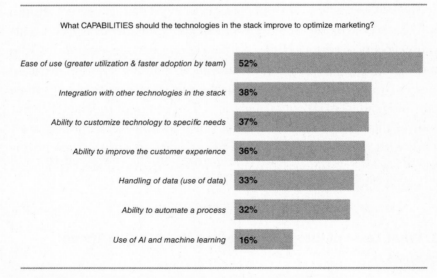

FIGURE 6.3   Integration with other stack technologies.

Source: From Martech Stack Optimization, Ascend2.

Let's say, for example, that I want to measure the lead to opportunity rate from a particular campaign to understand if the campaign was generating qualified leads that developed into opportunities. The two pieces of data that we need for that formula are:

$$\frac{\text{Lead conversions from that campaign}}{\text{Opportunities generated by that campaign}}$$

While marketers may have initial lead or conversion data in the marketing automation tool, they may not also have access in that same tool to which leads or contacts generated a sales opportunity. Sales opportunity data would be housed in the CRM tool, and if these two platforms do not communicate this data back and forth, marketers are left to access the data separately and recombine it outside of the platforms to combine the data and identify trends, which can be highly time consuming.

Ideally marketers need to quickly and easily assess the success of channels and campaigns. What's required for faster decision-making is a "single pane of glass" approach to allow marketers quick access to the data points they need. Vangie Beal at Webopedia describes the "single pane of glass" as "a management tool — such as a unified console or dashboard — that integrates information from varied sources across multiple applications and environments into a single display." Those data insights are what marketers crave from their martech stack today (see Figure 6.4).

4. What, If Any, Additional Transformation Do You Need to Perform on the Data?

It's important to think about the kind of intelligence you need first and then figure out where you can source that data and any kind of transformation that needs to be done to it. As marketers, you should not feel restricted by the limitations of a specific martech platform; out-of-the-box reporting is only the beginning, but too many people rely on what is meant to be generic enough to fit a wide range

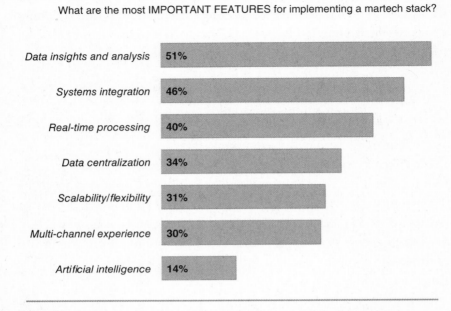

What are the most IMPORTANT FEATURES for implementing a martech stack?

Data insights and analysis	51%
Systems integration	46%
Real-time processing	40%
Data centralization	34%
Scalability/flexibility	31%
Multi-channel experience	30%
Artificial intelligence	14%

FIGURE 6.4   Marketers rank data insights and analysis as the most important feature in implementing the martech stack.

Source: From Martech Stack Optimization, Ascend2

of businesses when your business is unique. There are more visualization options now – additional modules that can be purchased and third-party tools – that are affordable for a wider range of businesses that will allow you to pull in data, do some kind of transformation, then either store that data or do the calculations on the fly in order to display what you need in reports and dashboards for marketing and sales management, the CEO, CFO, and so on.

One example of a metric that we have used that required data transformation is from the sales and marketing funnel. Depending on the platform that houses lead information by stage – marketing automation tool or CRM – you may need to purchase additional module functionality or create customizations in order to save a monthly count of number of leads for each stage. This is the first step for showing funnel metrics over time. These static counts of leads per stage per month, for example, can be plotted to show trends over time. An additional step is to show the percentage change over time by doing a simple calculation like this:

$$\frac{\text{Leads per Stage for Month} - \text{Leads per Stage for Prior Month}}{\text{Leads per Stage for Prior Month}}$$

Multiply by 100 and you get the percentage change per stage per month. This is a key metric for showing how marketing and sales is doing, and yet surprisingly one that's not readily available without some customization. Plotting these in a line graph shows trending for how quickly marketing/sales is doing better or worse over time instead of static data points. One more step: combine this percentage change/month trend line with conversion rate per stage and you have a very interesting graph that shows at a glance how adding more leads per stage may or may not affect conversion rate – always an area that marketers and salespeople should seek to optimize by becoming more efficient, creating new content, spending more resources and time, and the like.

5. How Will You Visualize This Information for the Stakeholders?

How you present data to communicate insights is just as important as the actual data that you are sharing. Because the size and complexity of the datasets we need to share and gain insight from are often so massive, data visualization helps our marketing teams to gain insights quickly and to communicate findings.

Inside of our marketing teams, visualization helps us to recognize trends and highlights quickly. For example, in organic search, we may have hundreds of keywords we track each month for rankings. Data visualization methods such as a conditional heat map formatting in Excel can quickly highlight keywords with the greatest improvements or those with the greatest drops (see Figure 6.5).

However, for our stakeholders, the way we visually present data may be even more critical. In a 2014 study from NYU, researchers

B	C	D	E	F	G	H
Keyword	Feb-20	Jan-20	Dec-19	Nov-19	Oct-19	Sep-19
Keyword 1	25	27	27	1	3	3
Keyword 2	20	32	32	79	87	87
Keyword 3	30	26	26	52	91	91
Keyword 4	3	5	5	29	44	44
Keyword 5	12	14	14	28	50	50
Keyword 6	91	79	79	11	8	8
Keyword 7	1	6	6	6	18	18
Keyword 8	19	23	23	31	47	47
Keyword 9	21	13	13	16	24	24
Keyword 10	40	35	35	1	1	1
Keyword 11	80	86	86	1	1	1
Keyword 12	78	95	95	31	33	33
Keyword 13	12	46	46	48	51	51
Keyword 14	45	49	49	15	18	18
Keyword 15	19	31	31	30	39	39
Keyword 16	50	64	64	14	35	35

FIGURE 6.5   Example of a Conditionally Formatted Heat Map in Microsoft Excel.

examined how visual data representation through charts versus textual data representation could sway participants' opinions. The researchers asked participants about to rate their agreement with certain statements about video games, such as "Violent video games do not contribute toward youth violence." The participants were then shown survey results that indicated the reasons kids said that they like to play video games. Some participants were shown a table of data, while others were presented with the data in graphical form.

After being presented with the new data, participants were again asked to rate their agreement with the same statements as before. Interestingly, even though the data presented to both groups was the same actual data, those that saw the visualized data through a chart exhibited a significantly higher change in their answers when presented with the visual data.

The NYU study demonstrates just how impactful data visualization can be at convincing others of a particular point. As marketers, we must think critically about the best ways to present data to stakeholders to ensure agreement and investment by stakeholders.

Today there are many tools that can help bring disparate systems together to combine and visualize data in a meaningful way. Google Data Studio, Microsoft Power BI, and Tableau are several of the data visualization platforms available. However even after you pull data from their original platforms, the data may still need adjustment to organize and visualize the data in a meaningful way. For example, Google Analytics provides dimensions (data attributes) and metrics (quantitative measurements). There are times you may want to flip your dimensions and metrics or display them in a different way.

For example, let's say that I want to create a simple pie chart showing how many goals were met on the site by organic search traffic in

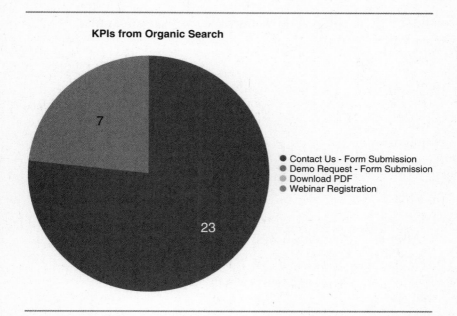

FIGURE 6.6   Example of a Pie Chart.

the past month, separated by goal. Because source/medium and each goal are dimensions in Google Analytics, you currently can't simply import this data into Google Data Studio and make one a dimension and one a metric.

However, as with all data, we can manipulate, combine and filter the data and then upload the information into our visualization tool to flip dimensions and metrics to achieve the desired result. Figure 6.6 illustrates a pie chart created by pulling KPI data from Google Analytics into Google Sheets, swapping the dimensions and metrics, and then importing into Google Data Studio to create the data visualization in the format we want, given that the data could not be produced this way directly from Google Analytics.

Take time with your visualizations and choose chart types that effectively communicate your message. Start with what you're trying to communicate and determine the right graph from there.

Data Being Shared	Possible Graph Types	
Comparing simple values	Column	Line
	Bar	Scatter Plot
	Pie	Bullet
Composition	Pie	Area
	Stacked Bar	Waterfall
	Stacked Column	
Distribution	Scatter Plot	Column
	Mekko	Bar
	Line	
Analyzing Trends	Line	Column
	Dual-Axis Line	
Relationships between Value Sets	Scatter Plot	Line
	Bubble	
Progression in the Sales Funnel	Funnel	
Progression towards a goal, like revenue	Bullet Graph	
Comparison between geographic regions	Geo Map	
Comparing data in tables quickly	Heat Map	

6. What Additional Tools and/or Technical or Developer Resources Do You Need to Accomplish This Goal?

Thankfully many tools today have built-in integrations, helping marketers to connect data across various platforms. For example, the marketing automation tool Marketo has an integration with Salesforce CRM. In other cases, however, where integrations do not exist between your data warehouses, you may need additional tools or technical resources to access the data you need.

When we chose a marketing automation tool, it included CRM functionality. However, after about a year of using the tool, we realized that because of the way that the marketing automation tool organized and stored the data, it was nearly impossible to pull out the data we needed in all the ways that we wanted to use it. Our old CRM tool, Salesforce, however, did have a structure we could adapt and modify to meet our needs. Even though Salesforce has an extensive integration marketplace with thousands of integration options, there was no existing integration between our marketing automation tool and Salesforce.

We turned to another tool – Zapier – to solve the integration problem. Zapier is an API integration tool that's easy to use even for those who may not be very technical or understand complex API programming. It allowed us to simply create integrations between our marketing automation tool and Salesforce CRM, thus allowing us to organize the marketing and sales data within Salesforce and help us achieve the reporting we desired in a malleable format.

If you can't find tools to enable your integrations, you may also need additional developer resources. Generally, the web developers in most organizations are part of the IT department, not the marketing team. This can make it difficult for marketing to get access to development resources since the marketing team finds itself competing with other departments for web developers' time.

When we choose a martech platform, an API can be a critical feature. Even if the platform doesn't provide all of the data innately and may not have existing integrations with your existing martech stack components, if the platform has an API then you can generally pull data into another platform for analysis and data sharing. For example, perhaps you have a custom CRM that your sales team uses. If your marketing automation platform has an API, you can engage a web developer to connect the marketing automation API to your custom CRM to pass lead information and associated data from the marketing automation tool to the CRM.

Just as CMOs are expected to align with business objectives and track efforts to achieve revenue, CIOs are under similar pressure. The IDG State of the CIO in 2020 reported that 67% of CIOs say that the creation of new revenue-generating initiatives is among their job responsibilities. Further, 46% said that they are creating business case scenarios with defined costs and benefits. Understanding the CIO's and IT department's priorities can help marketing to approach IT to get our projects worked on.

If you're facing pushback or delays due to IT backlog, ensure you've got a compelling business case for your web development resource needs that matches those of the CIO.

GET STARTED TODAY

Accessing and integrating data across the martech stack and other business data repositories is no simple task. However, understanding the data you have and where to access it is critical to marketing's success.

1. Know What Data You Need

Start off by listing out the data you need. What questions are you trying to answer? What measurements do you need to determine marketing success? What data do you need to answer these questions?

2. Map and Evaluate Your Current Data Sources

Once you know the data you need, determine where that data resides. Map out your data sources and the data they hold. You may likely find that your data resides in multiple locations, making it cumbersome to collect and combine.

3. Determine Where Holes Exist in Your Marketing Data Access and Address

In your martech map, what holes exist? Are there simple solutions to address these data chasms? Perhaps an additional tool is the answer. Evaluate your current gaps and determine which solutions may fit well with your existing martech infrastructure. As you evaluate new additions to your martech stack, consider how you'll need to access data, what kind of data you could collect, how you'll integrate data from the new tool into your existing tools, and what reporting features the tool may provide.

CHAPTER 7

Step 3: Data Analysis

Water, water everywhere / Nor any drop to drink.

– Samuel Taylor Coleridge, "The Rime of the Ancient Mariner"

Thanks to the digital economy, we are surrounded by data. Every martech platform we use generates a vast amount of information, yet for most of us, we use only a small portion of that data for reports or visualization. If you don't believe us, take a look at your marketing automation database. Run a report that pulls all fields for all leads and honestly ask yourself when was the last time you used more than a fraction of it for anything besides setting up your next email campaign or program.

The interface we see when we use something like a marketing automation tool is important; it helps us to interact with the vast amount of data underlying everything we are able to do in the tool. After all, that's what automation was designed for – to fulfill the promise of digital marketing of being able to reach, nurture, and filter through many times (100x, 1,000x, 10,000x) more leads than we could ever have done previously or manually. But the interface also puts us at an artificial remove from the data, and as a consequence many marketers rely only on the out-of-box reporting and never delve deeper for insights that are unique to their businesses and are not things that can be found by every other company using the same tool and the same reports.

The quote above refers to a sailor who is surrounded by salt water and is unable to drink any of it. If you can think about data as water, we are taking you on a journey in this book to help turn it from salt water to something you can actually consume.

Fortune 1000 companies can afford to hire data scientists to do marketing data analysis, and especially for B2C companies, the amount of data approaches or even reaches big data levels. Data scientists have specialized tools and utilize programming skills to handle analysis at this level. For the rest of us, a familiarity with Excel and martech platforms, in particular marketing automation and CRMs, can usually suffice. In addition, there are data visualization tools like Looker and Google Data Studio, which do not require a data scientist's help. Depending on the tools you are using and your visualization needs, you may want to get some consulting help for setup, but once the key metrics are defined and being pulled into customized reports and dashboards, you should only need occasional help when you have any additional requirements you cannot meet yourself.

This chapter focuses on the kind of analysis that data-first marketers should be able to do mostly on their own. Starting with the biases that we all – data scientists included – have to overcome when it comes to data analysis, we move on to the data fallacies that marketers, in particular, have a tendency to fall back on. Finally, we give some practical examples of marketing data analysis using the familiar sales and marketing funnel for lead nurturing with lead stages (e.g., MAL, MQL, SAL, and SQL) and how to glean insights for improving marketing performance and efficiency.

COGNITIVE BIASES: ONE MORE LESSON FROM MONEYBALL

In 1999, John Henry bought the Florida Marlins. Henry was a fan of Bill James and sabermetrics and had made his own fortune on Wall Street by taking advantage of inefficiencies in the market that statistical analysis could reveal. He wrote a letter to ESPN's Rob Neyer in which he drew parallels between the opportunities on Wall Street and the market for baseball players:

> People in both fields operate with beliefs and biases. To the extent you can eliminate both and replace them with data, you gain a clear advantage. . . . Actual data from the market means more than individual perception/belief. The same is true in baseball. (Lewis, 2003, p. 90)

Henry put his statistical skills to work and won his fantasy baseball league every year, but when it came to instituting this kind of change in his real-life baseball team, he failed, and the Marlins lost accordingly. Even though he himself believed in sabermetrics, he could not get past the perception/belief in the minds of those around him that how they chose baseball players was the way it was because it was the right way, the proven way, the way it had always been done.

Cognitive biases are a category of biases that human beings have evolved over time. Designed to actually help, they are also often an obstacle to overcome when it comes to data analysis:

> Cognitive biases are the result of our evolutionary process. They are designed to help us survive by making fast decisions in critical time sensitive situations and deal with limited information processing capabilities of human brain. Simply, they are the reason behind our *gut-feeling*. These biases can often cause irrational behaviour that goes against facts and lead to systematic errors in judgement. (Bysani, 2019)

In the *Moneyball* example above, Henry runs right into confirmation bias, a cognitive bias defined as the "human tendency to search for, favor, and use information that confirms one's pre-existing views on a certain topic" (Healy, 2016). Compounding the issue is the bandwagon effect, or "the tendency people have to adopt a certain behavior, style, or attitude simply because everyone else is doing it" (Cherry, 2019).

The scouts already know what attributes to look for in new talent; it's what they've always looked for. This is how everyone does it. Even faced with data that disproves the correlation of the factors that make up the basis of old scouting to actual wins, baseball management would not believe it. After years of writing the Baseball Abstract, Bill James gave up trying to convince baseball insiders who would not adopt what he was advising. The last of the original Baseball Abstracts was published in 1988, and it would be over a dozen years until an MLB team put what he wrote into practice, as shown in *Moneyball*.

EXAMPLE OF BEATING COGNITIVE BIASES: RELY ON DATA

FOSE, one of the oldest and largest IT conferences for the federal government, had a banner year in 2014: registrations were up 40% and more importantly, C-level executive registrations were up 25%. Yet a year later, after 37 years running, 1105 Media, the parent company of this show, announced that FOSE was dead.

We probably won't know all the reasons why the parent company killed the show – management changes, new priorities, new events – but there's one thing that many people say: "It was a long time coming."

For years, FOSE had had a bad reputation. People said that real government IT decision makers did not come to the show; instead they sent their assistants, who took advantage of some time out of the office to go shopping for free "tchotchkes" that the vendors handed out. In fact, some exhibitors handed out branded plastic shopping bags, which just reinforced this belief.

FOSE was the first tradeshow at which ScienceLogic was an exhibitor. It was local, relatively inexpensive, and the largest IT show for the federal government, a key market for our young company. Because of the rumors, we did the work preshow to send targeted invitations to decision makers to visit our booth and pick up the latest Wallace and Gromit video. Instead of ignoring the rumors, we decided to take advantage of them. People go to conferences and bring things back for their kids; we just wanted to add more incentive for actual buyers to come by. We also saw everyone else, or the "shoppers," as potential influencers in future sales, so we invested in branded but inexpensive tchotchkes that we were more than happy to hand out. That invite-only offer brought some surprising people to our booth, including the CIO of the Treasury Department, and after just a few years of exhibiting at FOSE, we were showing a 40,000% ROI. In this case, we made the confirmation bias and bandwagon effect work for us. If we had only believed everyone else, we never would have done the show. When we took a step back and actually looked at the opportunity to reach not just influencers but also buyers in a notoriously tough market, we thought FOSE was worth it, and the numbers proved us right.

OVERCOMING BIASES AND BELIEFS

Marketing intelligence derived from data does not happen in a vacuum. There is no magic black box into which you dump all of your data, then, presto, out come insights for new products, better campaigns, more targeting. This is the good news. Even if you have the budget to hire data scientists, our experience as marketers is critical to:

1. Ask the right questions.
2. Define the factors (and data) that will help to answer the questions.
3. Interpret the results in meaningful and actionable ways.

The not-as-good news is that every time you inject a human – you – into analytics, you have to deal with the "beliefs and biases" that Henry wrote about in that letter. This is not a judgment; it holds true for all human beings. What we do and how we think are molded by our experiences, beliefs, and biases. Some are glass-half-full people; others see the glass as half empty. It's very difficult to overcome our biases and instead rely on "objective" actual data, especially since even the data we select to analyze can be "biased."

Sometimes when we fear something new, we fall back on what we already know, and for most marketers that is not analyzing data. As we've said, this is not an easy transformation. If it were easy, everyone would do it, and then it wouldn't be a competitive advantage.

For the marketers who accept the data-first challenge, let's explore some of the more prevalent cognitive biases and data fallacies that you should try to overcome and avoid when it comes to analyzing data.

Belief: Form Over Function, or "Look How Pretty My Website Is"

Opening the box for a new Apple device is always a pleasure. The packaging is perfect; the components, from the minimal instructions to the device itself to the power cord, adaptor, and any other peripherals, are always laid out in the correct order. Even without the instructions, it seems intuitive. It just makes sense. This is an example of how form follows function.

On the other hand, we have some high-profile website cautionary tales where form seemed to trump function. Let's be real; we can all agree that when it comes to a website, functionality is the priority. Getting a visitor to become a customer is the number one goal on an ecommerce site. So why do websites fail to achieve this goal, some rather spectacularly?

Finish Line's Costly Website Redesign

In 2012, retailer Finish Line decided to redo their website (see Figure 7.1) – not a bad idea, if they had not made several mistakes along the way. One of the people involved in the redesign thought the new site should be nominated for Most Improved Website of All Time, praising the design as "pretty." Instead of showing athletic shoes and some apparel and accessories, the home page now showed a blow-up photo of the face of an attractive twenty-something guy (see Figure 7.2). If you looked at the new home page, you would have no idea what this site was actually for – which was to sell athletic shoes.

FIGURE 7.1   Finish Line Home Page Before Redesign.
Source: Finish Line, Inc.

To make matters worse, Finish Line launched their new site just days before the holiday shopping season kicked off. In the 17 days the new site was up, Finish Line lost $3 million in revenue and analysts downgraded the stock from buy rating to hold as well as lowering stock price targets (Schouten, 2012). Executive heads rolled, including the chief digital officer. In December, they reverted to their old site and platform. Finish Line's postmortem with the CEO and president concluded that traffic was actually up on the site but faulty site design and functionality had caused issues with the overall customer experience (Blair, 2013), which in turn lowered conversion rates.

Launching a new ecommerce platform right before the biggest shopping season of the year is never a good idea, but more than that, this website redesign illustrates a trap that marketers in particular are partial to. Making something look attractive is in our marketing DNA; we are taught to conform to prevailing design aesthetics at any given time, usually defined by Madison Avenue. But form over function is

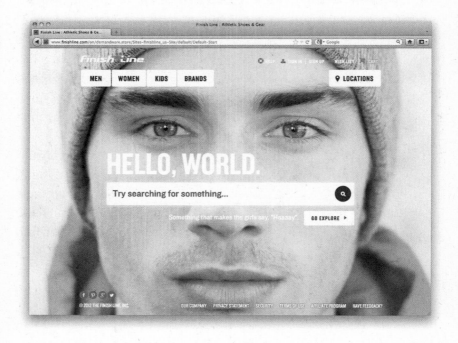

FIGURE 7.2   Finish Line Home Page - After Redesign. What Does Finish Line Do to Make the Girls Go Haaaaay?
Source: Finish Line, Inc.

always a mistake and one we make because sometimes we lose track of what's really important. It's not about making something you'd be proud to submit for a marketing/advertising award; it's about achieving business goals. If the business goal is to sell more athletic shoes, then form and function need to support that, and data will help us prove it. Don't be scared of data and don't ignore it to make a site "pretty"; in the case of the Finish Line website, the numbers showed them the potential revenue loss caused by lower conversion rates, and it made them act quickly to preserve the rest of the holiday season revenue.

Marks & Spencer Backs Out Website Because of the Numbers

The Finish Line story is pretty bad, but this one may top it. In February 2014, after almost two years and £150m ($240 million), Marks & Spencer launched a new website and ecommerce platform (McGarvey, 2014). In the first 13 weeks, the company's online sales dropped 8%. At least it didn't make the mistake that Finish Line did and launch the new site right in time for the big holiday shopping season; it had time to correct any problems.

A big part of the redesign was bringing more video and magazine-style content to the site (Rankin, 2014). There's nothing wrong with doing that, but once again, what should have been most important was not engaging visitors with content and making the site "pretty" but instead focusing on actually turning a browser into a customer and, in particular, removing any obstacles to making that happen. For any ecommerce site, converting customers must be the number one goal – from a business and marketing perspective. The new site reportedly did just the opposite: people had problems registering, there were site crashes, customers found it hard to navigate, and they couldn't find what they wanted (Fernando, 2014).

The company made changes to the website platform and by the first quarter of 2015, online sales were back up by 38.7%. Despite all of this turmoil and lost revenue, the lead designer of the new site called it a successful launch that "repositioned M&S as a trend-led fashion shopping site that inspires customers with outfitting ideas and carefully curated editorial contents." Clearly, he wasn't looking at the numbers.

Availability Bias: Look at All the Data

One more bias is very relevant as marketers begin to do more analysis themselves. Availability bias has us making judgments based on what most quickly comes to mind – in the case of data, the metrics that we can immediately think of. Two caveats here for marketers:

- First, selecting the right data to build your case/answer your questions is very important and something that may change over time. Sometimes (fewer than we would like), doing so may be straightforward; all the data you need is contained in your CRM, for example, and it's just a matter of generating an out-of-the-box report with appropriate filters. Example: A report on all revenue generated in the last year from marketing-sourced leads. Of course, this means leads must all be marked correctly with original lead source and that original lead source is a "marketing" one (which may require a custom field to designate) and then those leads are all associated with the correct opportunities. The full explanation of what you need to do may be even longer than this depending on your martech stack and data setup, but it can absolutely be done if the metrics and sales/marketing processes are put in place to ensure you get the data you need. Most times, however, this is not as straightforward, such as if some of the data you need sits in different databases, if you don't have access to those other sources, or if you need to define custom reporting because out-of-the-box is meant to be generic and your business is not.
- Second, what if you don't even know the other source exists because it's not a "marketing" database, but one that IT or Finance has set up? When you are setting up what data you need to answer your questions, it's important to take a step back and think about what your "ideal" set of data would be and not be limited to what is readily available. Once you do know, you can do what you have to get access, if possible, or as stated above, create processes that will produce the data you really need. That, plus constant questioning if you have the right data, will get you past the availability bias.

Data Fallacies to Avoid

Data fallacies are common pitfalls that people encounter when analyzing data. For the purposes of our discussion, we have chosen two data fallacies that marketers are particularly prone to fall prey to.

Cherry Picking

Logically Fallacious defines cherry-picking as "ignoring inconvenient data, suppressed evidence, fallacy of incomplete evidence, argument by selective observation, argument by half-truth, card stacking, fallacy of exclusion, ignoring the counter evidence, one-sided assessment, slanting, one-sidedness." In other words, don't do it. Basically, it happens when you select only the data to support an outcome you want – perhaps something you want to say or how you want to be perceived – and willfully ignore the rest.

Everyone wants to look good. When the time comes around to do reports for the board meeting, choosing metrics that make marketing look good is a dangerous temptation. Let's go back to that website traffic metric. If Finish Line had just shown that metric to executives, the redesign would make marketing look like heroes – initially. In fact, traffic was up but conversion was down, and in the end, revenue was below what it should have been by millions of dollars. If they never looked at the conversion number, they wouldn't have known just how bad the problem was. Cherry-picking is a shortsighted tactic that will be found out.

False Causality or Correlation Is not Causation

There is a very funny graphic on Spurious Correlations that shows clearly false correlations. Figure 7.3 is our favorite and shows that if we could just keep Nicolas Cage from getting any roles, people would stop drowning by falling into pools!

So, if we could just keep Nicolas Cage from getting any roles, people would stop drowning by falling into pools (see Figure 7.3)! Obviously, this overstates the case, but the point is valid, which is that just because two events occur together, it does not mean that one caused the other.

To think that data analysis is "objective" is not realistic. Data must be understood in context. As marketers, we should already know the factors that can most impact performance of an email, for example. After all, we design an email campaign with those factors in mind – subject, content, day, time of day, frequency, targeted list, offer, and so on. Therefore, analyzing performance across multiple

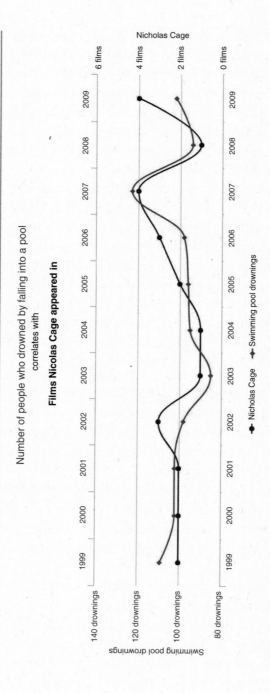

Number of people who drowned by falling into a pool
correlates with

Films Nicolas Cage appeared in

FIGURE 7.3 False Causality.

Source: Chart created by Tyler Vigen as part of his Spurious Correlations project, http://www.tylervigen.com/spurious-correlations.

campaigns using these factors to see any kind of correlation should be valid, with caveats, such as making sure we select the right factors and have enough data to draw conclusions.

Done right, marketing analysis is not just a single conclusion but a series of them. In this case, the scientific method absolutely applies. Here's an example of applying the scientific method to an email campaign (see Figure 7.4), then gleaning insights from performance metrics and running the "experiment" again, to hopefully better results. And if not to better results, that's just more data to analyze for the next campaign.

Scientific Method Step	Email Campaign: Performance The "Experiment"
Observation/Question	Email invites for a recent webinar were sent on a staggered schedule. The audience was all part of a single targeted segment, but registrations varied by day.
Hypothesis	Emails sent on Tuesday/Thursday perform better than those sent on Monday/Friday.
Experimentation	Follow the same staggered schedule for the next webinar invite.
Data Analysis	Do we see any pattern in registrations?
Conclusion	We do see a better click-through rate to the landing page for webinar registration, but it's unclear that actual registration changes based on a specific day. We need to do more testing.
and Repeat . . .	

FIGURE 7.4 **Example of Applying the Scientific Method to an Email Campaign.**

ANALYZING DIFFERENT TYPES OF MARKETING DATA

You can define data used by marketing in various ways – internal versus external, click-based, social-media based, and so on – but for the purposes of this book, let's look at two categories, customer data and marketing operations data.

1. Customer Data

Customer data is usually the information that can be found in your marketing automation tool, CRM, and/or website tracking tools such as Google Analytics. This includes demographic information in addition to behavior-based data, such as content accessed, pages visited, and even products purchased. Ideally, you can track each marketing touch for each lead from the first time they hit your site or show up in your database all the way through to purchase. There is some work needed to track these touches and tie them to individuals for digital campaigns, but for many offline campaigns, like events or sales line calls, you may need to do manual reconciliation.

These individual buyer journeys can be analyzed in aggregate for insights that help to create buyer personas, such as director or VP of marketing in small to medium enterprises, which in turn help marketing to build target audiences for ads, content, events, and the like. For B2B businesses, the "customer" is a business and not an individual, and marketing can mine customer data, with individuals grouped into their businesses, for additional intelligence, such as differentiating purchasers from influencers and making any correlations from buying role to titles or function.

There are many ways to slice and dice this kind of information, but one filter that you should always be looking at is revenue-based. Look at revenue or purchases in terms of lead source, industry, time to buy, how many touches until conversion, and so on. And perhaps equally important is looking at the opposite – abandoned carts or opportunities to close lost – and trying to divulge patterns or commonalities, in particular areas in which marketing can improve its own activities or help sales to close deals.

2. Marketing Operations Data

Marketing operations data is the information that marketing collects on the performance of campaigns or programs. Ideally, this information can be collected and/or accessed across all channels and martech tools or platforms that are used, creating a unified view of data from multiple sources.

Marketing operations data can overlap with customer data when it comes to click-based data (e.g., content accessed), but instead of creating a view of buyers, the purpose of analyzing marketing operations data is to increase marketing efficiency by identifying key factors in campaigns that perform well, eliminating poorly performing campaigns, and decreasing the friction between stages of the sales and marketing funnel, ultimately to increase sales/revenue.

Data Analysis Example: Marketing Performance and Efficiency

Let's take a closer look at the marketing and sales funnel used by B2B companies to show what we mean by analyzing marketing operations data to improve marketing performance and efficiency.

MAL: Marketing Accepted Lead. Unqualified leads that first enter your lead-nurturing process.

MQL: Marketing Qualified Lead. MALs that have reached a predefined threshold of interaction/engagement with your website/assets/ emails to say they are "interested."

SAL: Sales Accepted Lead. "Handoff" from marketing working the leads to sales actively working these leads for further qualification.

SQL: Sales Qualified Lead. Sales opportunity defined with budget, potential revenue, time to purchase, and so on.

Customer: Opportunities to close won.

FIGURE 7.5   Sample Sales and Marketing Funnel with Lead Nurturing Stages Defined.

Often data is shown as a snapshot in time – daily, weekly, monthly. Goals are often set up this way as well. *Our target is 100 new marketing qualified leads this month. I want 500 leads generated from this ad campaign.* Counts are straightforward metrics, but like any data it needs to be understood in context, and one of those contexts is measured against itself to show trends. *Am I doing better this month than last month? And overall am I doing better at generating quality leads over the last year?*

When it comes to the sales and marketing funnel, marketers often look at their numbers from month to month to get an idea of how many leads (MAL) we need to stuff into the top of the funnel to achieve revenue targets at the bottom of the funnel. Estimating this number is predicated on an understanding of what the conversion rate is from one stage of the funnel to the next.

Measuring the conversion rate, in particular, allows marketing to benchmark against itself; it's a metric that when shown in a trended line illustrates marketing efficiency improvement from month to month – for marketing management and the C-suite. Let's show some examples of funnel graphs.

All these graphs are generated from an Excel spreadsheet. These are just a few ways to take a single dataset of funnel metrics over the period of one year and start to do analysis.

Lead Nurturing: Number of Leads

The graph in Figure 7.6 shows the number of leads in each defined stage of the sales and marketing funnel, or the lead-nurturing process. In one image, we can see the number of leads, but more importantly

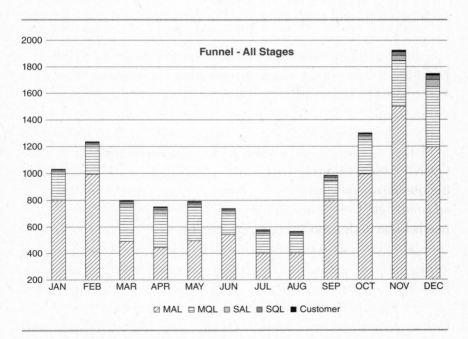

FIGURE 7.6   Stacked Graph: Number of Leads by Stage over Time.

we can start to see trends – perhaps seasonality, for instance. It looks like summer is a relatively slower time for adding new leads into the funnel and working them, while we see a big boost in the fall and especially into the holiday season. In this case, the data matches the narrative because we know that the holiday season and the end of the year is a critical time for sales, and the business and marketing efforts are ramped up accordingly. Perhaps the other thing we see is some big trade shows that are always good for a quick increase of MALs, such as in February.

The other thing a stacked graph like this shows quickly is the difference between numbers of leads added to each stage for the month and overall how that difference changes over time. MAL is the beginning but those are unqualified leads. The focus instead should be how well we are doing once we get those leads in the door, and perhaps it's also a reflection of how well we are targeting MALs that we bring in, relatively speaking. Despite the slowdown in new MALs starting in March, we're actually doing better at qualifying these leads and moving them to sales, where it looks like sales is also doing better at qualifying them, indicating possibly that the quality of the leads is high. We see the same bump at the end of the year, and that rates taking a closer look at what we did right before the bump and during it (i.e., looking at specific campaigns that could be the cause).

Now let's take look at two alternative ways of looking at this data. As with marketing itself, it takes some experimentation to find the right fit for what we are trying to do, or in this case, what we are trying to most effectively show.

Conversion Rate and Percentage Change

Instead of counts and trends for each lead stage shown in a stacked graph, this one focuses on two important trends that can be shown from the same dataset with the addition of one more stage, "Customer," after SQL; that is what we are after here (see Figure 7.7). *Conversion rate* shows movement of leads from one stage to the next one (e.g., MQL to SQL conversion rate, which is usually defined as the handoff from marketing to sales). *How quickly are we moving*

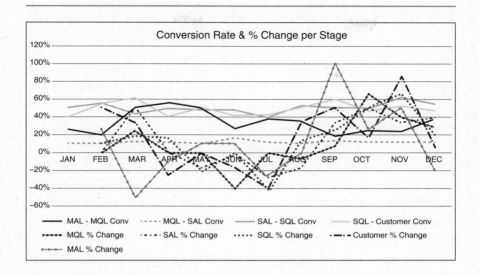

FIGURE 7.7 **Line Graph: Conversion Rate and Percentage Change by Stage.**

leads through the funnel? Here's the calculation:

$$\frac{\text{Leads per Stage for Month} - \text{Leads per Stage for Prior Month}}{\text{Leads per Stage for Prior Month}}$$

The second metric shown here is percent change per stage, so this is the trend line from the first graph but shown as a percentage to more easily compare it to the conversion rate so we can see if there are any correlations to make or areas of more investigation. We are showing all stages in the graph above but feel free to chunk this up to make it easier on the eyes. There are a lot of observations we could make here, but as with all things data, it is always a good idea to keep trying to prove and disprove causation. Some observations:

• The rate at which sales qualified leads (SQLs) become customers remains pretty steady at around 50%, despite relatively big variations in how many leads are added to any given stage.

- In fact, all of the conversion rates look relatively flat except for the first – MAL to MQL. This could be a factor of the amount of "garbage" leads that come in through various sources; after all, these are unqualified leads, but it could also be an area we want to take a closer look at because it may mean we are doing a better job with targeting in certain activities versus others.
- That big dip in MAL percentage change in March and the big increase in September follows our marketing activities, but it might be interesting in particular to compare to the year prior. Did we do the same activities/campaigns last year, and are we seeing the same dips and increases, or could there be something else affecting this we don't know about?

Now let's look at the same metrics but as a bar graph (see Figure 7.8).

Visualizing the information this way allows us to more readily see the highs and the lows, and especially every time the rates dip. It also shows everything at a glance in a more organized way. You might use

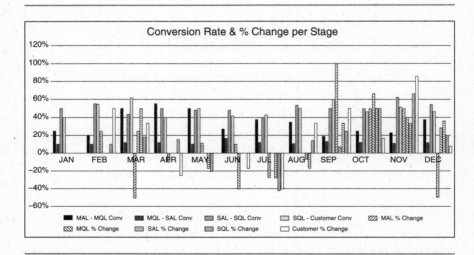

FIGURE 7.8   Bar Graph: Conversion Rate and Percentage Change by Stage.

this kind of graph for the aggregate view but use the line graphs for a subset of the data – for example, focusing in on certain parts of the funnel to better be able to view trends.

As we isolate the SAL/SQL/Customer conversion and change rates (see Figure 7.9), we can more easily see possible correlations.

- The conversion rates hold fairly steady over the course of the year, but as we look more closely we can see that the peaks occur as we also speed up adding SALs and SQLs – except in May and the end of the year. What else could be affecting this? Could time to close be another factor here?
- The end-of-year trend lines don't seem to match the patterns seen earlier in the year. Is this something specific to the holiday season? Can we identify any sales or marketing activities/actions that may account for this?

And finally, let's look at revenue.

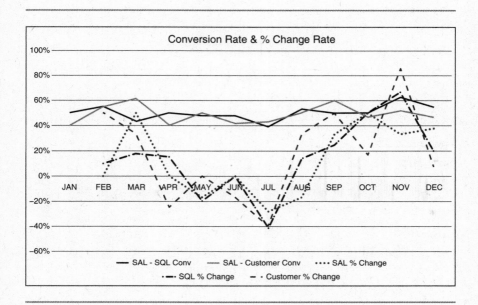

FIGURE 7.9 SAL/SQL and SQL/Customer Conversion Rate and Percentage Change.

Marketing-Sourced: Pipeline and Revenue

This graph shows pipeline added, revenue won, and revenue lost from marketing sourced leads (see Figure 7.10). It is shown here as a stacked graph so that you can also see at a glance the overall revenue pool in play each month.

- It's not surprising that the biggest revenue pool is at the end of the year during the holiday season and perhaps into January as a carryover, but what is happening in June? Revenue lost far outweighs added pipeline and revenue won, but is this a fluke? What makes up that $80,000 in lost revenue? Is it because of one big lost deal, or is this several deals and something we need to be more concerned about?

- At a glance, this graph shows relative amounts in each revenue category; September through December show great trends. Not only is the revenue lost relatively low in those months, but pipeline, revenue won, and revenue pool are all trending up.

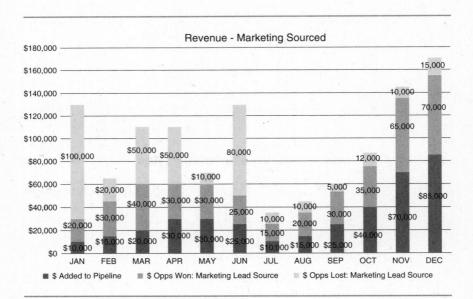

FIGURE 7.10   Stacked Graph: Revenue Attributed to Marketing Sources.

We have only shown five graphs here, and that's just working off of funnel data. There are far more permutations to play with, especially when it comes to revenue. Try slicing and dicing your data by channel, by lead source, by content asset, and so on. If you have set up data collection and integration correctly, you should be able to do all of this. Have fun with it, and believe that you have the right experience to ask the right questions and experiment when it comes to getting the answers.

GET STARTED TODAY

Don't be scared to start analyzing the data you have. Just because you haven't done it before doesn't mean you cannot do it. As the marketer who understands the what, how, and why of campaigns, you are ideally positioned to pull out the insights from the data generated by the campaigns. And the more you do it, the more you'll be comfortable doing it.

1. Keep Marketing Metrics Consistent from One Reporting Period to the Next

How will you know if you are doing better or worse over time if you don't actually measure consistently over time? If you believe a metric is important to the business and/or the marketing team, then you need to show it.

2. Experiment with Graph/Visualization Styles

A picture is worth a thousand words. Just changing from a line graph to a bar graph, for example, could surface insights you might not have seen otherwise.

3. Keep Experimenting

Keep asking questions. And remember always to ask why. The first answer is just that: the first. Consider other factors and don't be afraid to rework the question.

4. Always Keep the End Goal in Sight

Whether it's showing marketing's value to the business (marketing-sourced revenue) or looking at marketing operations data to identify critical areas of improvement (funnel conversion rates versus funnel percentage change rate), stay focused on your end goal.

CHAPTER 8

Step 4: The Data-First Marketing Campaign Framework

The Data-First Marketing Campaign Framework focuses on continuous improvement to help marketing organizations achieve the overarching business goals. To truly improve on a continuum, marketing campaigns must be treated as cycles, where marketing teams develop, execute, and then analyze the campaigns to learn what could improve them.

Campaigns represent the meat of marketing implementation, and it's often what external audiences associate with the work of marketing. While strategy and planning are the foundation to our marketing efforts, others see the product of our labors in the content and campaigns we create. But as marketers, we know that the content we develop and the campaigns we execute are a product of the strategy and plan we've created to meet our business marketing goals.

All too often, though, campaign execution does not bolster the overall business goals. There are so many opportunities available to marketers today – between new platforms, new platform features, new ad delivery options, and new creative execution – and there are new opportunities arising every day. Without a solid business marketing strategy and marketing plan, how can a marketer truly know which marketing opportunities present the best bets to achieving the business and marketing goals?

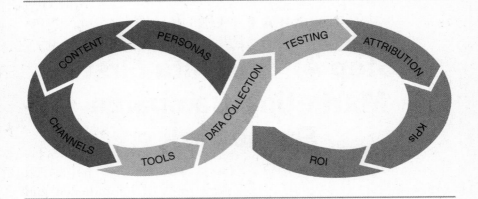

FIGURE 8.1   The Data-First Marketing Campaign Framework.

In this chapter we review the nine parts of the Data-First Marketing Campaign Framework. The framework is designed to encompass a continuous improvement model while always keeping sight of the overarching business goals and the importance of using data throughout to craft better campaigns with measurable performance and value. As shown in Figure 8.1, there are three main phases of the campaign framework: Development, Execution, and Analysis, and each of these main phases has three steps.

DEVELOPMENT PHASE

Abraham Lincoln said, "Give me six hours to chop down a tree and I will spend the first four sharpening the axe." Effective execution relies on thorough preparation. In this case, our preparation includes gathering information, creating content assets, and determining the appropriate channels for the campaign. While preparation doesn't always seem exciting or sexy to marketers, it does lay the groundwork for success throughout the marketing effort.

The Data-First Marketing Campaign Framework begins with just such preparation in the Development Phase. Laying the groundwork for our campaign requires three steps:

1. Build buyer personas.
2. Develop content assets.
3. Choose distribution and communication channels.

First, we must understand the people we are marketing to. As Jay Acunzo, the author of *Break the Wheel*, says, "You would never feed salad to a lion." In other words, we have to know our audience, and lions really don't prefer salad. If we want to gain new customers, it helps to understand who our customers are – what demographics they share and what their pain points are and what they're looking for. By starting with this foundational step, we compile important data that informs what prospects want to know from our businesses and what channels we can use to communicate with them.

1. Build Your Buyer Personas

The first step to a successful data-first marketing campaign is understanding the target audience. Building the buyer personas that match your target audience saves time and money and moves you closer to your ultimate goal of producing revenue faster. According to Peter Drucker, "The aim of marketing is to know and understand the customer so well the product or service fits him and sells itself."

Thoroughly understanding the buyer and the buyer journey are critical to planning and executing campaigns. Which types of content will a buyer be most responsive to? Which platforms are best to reach our target audience? When, where, and how long should these campaigns run? The buyer persona helps shape and define the content, channels, and methodologies used throughout a campaign to reach a prospect and convert that prospect to a lead or sale.

However, buyer personas should not be created solely in the vacuum of the marketing team, but rather involve other key stakeholders who also work with customers. Adele Revella, founder of the Buyer Persona Institute and author of *Buyer Personas: How to Gain Insight into Your Customer's Expectations, Align Your Marketing Strategies, and Win More Business*, shares the importance of having a shared understanding with the sales team of these key personas:

> As marketers gain familiarity with each of the people involved in the buying decision, as well as the steps they take and the factors they evaluate, they can help sales anticipate the inevitable obstacles and prepare the tools and arguments that sales needs to move these decisions along. There's another outcome that is just as critical, though. When marketing and sales share the same understanding about the work that's required to win more business, the gap between the two organizations closes and they naturally become a more cohesive and effective team. (Revella, 2015)

Key to Revella's approach in building buyer personas is an agreement with the sales team on buyer persona definitions. While marketers have some knowledge about the identity of prospects, in many cases, marketing may only have a portion of the data about who the actual buyers are and what led them to purchase. The sales team, and often the customer service team, also have valuable insights to provide and should be included in the buyer persona building process.

As a marketer, have you ever delivered many leads to the sales team only to have them reply that the leads are not good? It's a common situation for many marketers. In addition to acting as a campaign guideline for marketers, building buyer personas with the sales team helps create a standard definition and understanding between key stakeholders. In the buyer journey, who defines what qualifies a lead as "sales qualified"? Is the sales team actually helping to define their qualification requirements? They should be. Often those qualification requirements involve specific demographics or behavior. If the marketing team, however, does not have full view of sales data, how can the marketing team adequately define on its own what leads qualify to be the best sales prospects and become sales qualified leads?

According to LinkedIn's "State of Sales 2018" report, while 44% of marketing and sales professionals are working more closely together than in past years, only 20% of sales professionals report that sales and marketing significantly overlap to target leads. This misalignment between the two teams leads to quality disparity with leads, because sales' definition of quality may not match the definition by the marketing team. In the LinkedIn study, only 22% reported that leads from marketing were excellent and only 42% said lead quality was good.

Often termed the "sales and marketing handshake," an orchestrated approach between the marketing and sales teams, serves to benefit sales. Research shows that coordinated efforts between the marketing and sales teams don't just benefit marketing – they also benefit the sales team, which is financially incentivized to achieve sales goals. The trend of marketing and sales working closer together has certainly grown in recent years, and 57% of top sales performers (those who exceeded their sales targets by at least 25%) rank the importance of working with marketing at an eight out of ten or higher.

2. Develop Content Assets

While content marketing is a growing field, it's vital that marketers examine why we're creating content. Content creation is often one of the most difficult tasks of any organization, requiring expertise and resource investment. According to the 2017 study "Content Marketing and Distribution" from Ascend2, only 18% of organizations fulfill their content marketing needs solely in-house. Access to internal resources and the expertise of these resources often poses a challenge to fulfilling content needs. This makes it imperative to get the content mix, plan, and execution as accurate as possible, whether employing scarce internal resources or investing in external content creation services.

Once we understand the audience and we're targeting using the buyer persona, we can begin to create content that will attract and engage them. To begin, consider what questions are asked along the buyer journey, which can inform them along the path. Here, too, sales should be involved in marketing's planning efforts for content. Sales requires content that maps to the buyer journey to help answer questions and reduce friction. However, all too often content created by the sales and marketing teams separately also appear misaligned and can impact customers' brand perception. In the 2018 LinkedIn study, 89% of decision makers say consistent marketing and sales language about a product is "very important" (50%) or "important" (39%). Nearly half (48%), however, say they often or always experience different messaging from sales and marketing when learning about a solution.

When I (co-author Janet) give workshops on search engine optimization, I often give the example of how a buyer's search queries change along the journey. For example, someone looking to purchase running shoes may have search queries beginning with terms such as "women's running shoes" in the discovery phase on to more specific queries as the prospective buyer narrows the search (see Figure 8.2).

While this is a simplified view of the buyer journey, it illustrates that specific words may be searched along the journey. Additionally,

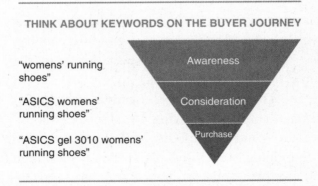

THINK ABOUT KEYWORDS ON THE BUYER JOURNEY

"womens' running shoes" — Awareness

"ASICS womens' running shoes" — Consideration

"ASICS gel 3010 womens' running shoes" — Purchase

FIGURE 8.2   Example of How Search Keywords Map to a Buyer's Journey.

buyers have questions along the journey. Just as the diagram represents keywords, it could just as easily represent the typical questions that buyers have along the journey.

In some cases, there may be more than one buyer persona for a product or service. For example, the human resources department in an organization will often enlist the assistance of the IT department to assess and approve an HR software purchase. In this scenario, there are two buyer personas: the HR department, with its requirements specific to HR use, and the IT department, assessing the software for compatibility, stability, and more. The HR personas will likely have very different questions when assessing the software than the IT personas will.

Also consider the goals of the content as they relate to the buyer journey stage. Content in the awareness and consideration stage may be used to establish brand, inform or educate while in the conversion or qualification stages may be designed to convince and convert. The stage of the buyer cycle will determine the subject of the content and the format that content takes.

Another consideration for content development is the planned channel for campaign execution. How will this piece of content be distributed? Via email? Through paid advertising? Through organic search? Depending on the content's buyer stage focus, the channel chosen for content distribution also helps determine how the content should be formatted. Should it be long-form or short-form content? Should it be easily digestible and visual, like an infographic, or should it be a highly textual and downloadable, like a whitepaper?

Jeff Gregory, SEO analyst for CustomInk, shared their three gauges that they use to conceive and measure content:

1. Traffic
2. Links
3. Conversions

Gregory explains, "We always ask ourselves: Will it get traffic, links, or conversions?" If content achieves traffic, that's considered good, and if it achieves links or conversions, that's great. Achieving traffic plus either links or conversions is even better. To achieve all three – traffic, links and conversions – is what Gregory describes as the trifecta. "The trifecta is always the supreme goal, but it's admittedly a rare occurrence."

Several years ago, we worked with a storage facility aggregator site. While so many others had trouble in creating meaningful content, this website did an amazing job at writing consequential articles on its blog related to the needs of its buyer personas. The articles were effective at ranking highly for related organic search terms and thereby generating high levels of organic search traffic to the site's blog.

On the surface, this story sounds like a wonderful success. The organization wrote content, optimized it for organic search, and drove significant website traffic from organic search. And it is a wonderful success story if the business marketing goal was to simply generate website traffic. But website traffic alone does not generate revenue.

Upon further analysis of the top blog posts for the first half of the year, the blog post with the most organic traffic produced over 17,000 new site visitors, but no visitors to that page booked a storage facility on the site (see Figure 8.3). The top five organic traffic-generating blog posts over that time did not generate even one web booking, even though they directed over 63,000 new site visitors from organic search.

While the new site traffic is clearly impressive, which metric is the CEO more concerned about: site traffic or web bookings?

Not all content or campaigns may result in a direct lead conversion, sales qualified lead, opportunity, or sale either. A great deal of content and campaigns may influence conversion, opportunity, and sale, but they may not be receiving any credit for this influence. Brand marketing is a good example of content and campaigns that may be intended to establish expertise or surface your product during the discovery phase. And often brand campaigns may not have a conversion metric associated with them.

Landing Page	Acquisition			Behavior			Conversions Goal 1: Web Booking ▾		
	Users ↓	New Users	Sessions	Bounce Rate	Pages / Session	Avg. Session Duration	Web Booking (Goal 1 Conversion Rate)	Web Booking (Goal 1 Completions)	Web Booking (Goal 1 Value)
	292,854 % of Total: 10.66% (2,747,113)	283,387 % of Total: 10.37% (2,732,304)	317,664 % of Total: 8.85% (3,588,444)	88.45% Avg for View: 56.84% (55.62%)	1.23 Avg for View: 2.35 (-47.90%)	00:00:44 Avg for View: 00:02:07 (-65.66%)	0.02% Avg for View: 2.11% (-98.82%)	78 % of Total: 0.10% (75,704)	$0.00 % of Total: 0.00% ($0.00)
1.	18,134 (6.08%)	17,890 (6.31%)	18,910 (5.95%)	95.25%	1.06	00:00:19	0.00%	0 (0.00%)	$0.00 (0.00%)
2.	12,841 (4.30%)	12,504 (4.41%)	13,861 (4.36%)	95.13%	1.08	00:00:25	0.00%	0 (0.00%)	$0.00 (0.00%)
3.	12,274 (4.11%)	12,065 (4.26%)	12,891 (4.06%)	91.03%	1.16	00:00:29	0.00%	0 (0.00%)	$0.00 (0.00%)
4.	11,505 (3.86%)	11,369 (4.01%)	12,324 (3.88%)	80.66%	1.28	00:01:02	0.00%	0 (0.00%)	$0.00 (0.00%)
5.	9,825 (3.29%)	9,660 (3.41%)	10,600 (3.34%)	93.77%	1.10	00:00:26	0.00%	0 (0.00%)	$0.00 (0.00%)
6.	9,379 (3.14%)	9,013 (3.18%)	9,940 (3.13%)	94.87%	1.09	00:00:28	0.00%	0 (0.00%)	$0.00 (0.00%)
7.	8,884 (2.98%)	8,295 (2.93%)	9,581 (3.02%)	87.17%	1.21	00:00:49	0.00%	0 (0.00%)	$0.00 (0.00%)
8.	8,467 (2.84%)	8,388 (2.96%)	9,322 (2.93%)	89.29%	1.19	00:00:45	0.00%	0 (0.00%)	$0.00 (0.00%)
9.	8,367 (2.80%)	8,072 (2.85%)	8,712 (2.74%)	79.38%	1.53	00:01:21	0.00%	0 (0.00%)	$0.00 (0.00%)
10.	8,345 (2.80%)	7,713 (2.72%)	8,762 (2.76%)	87.71%	1.19	00:00:49	0.00%	0 (0.00%)	$0.00 (0.00%)

FIGURE 8.3 Google Analytics of Top Blog Posts.

Don't just create content for the sake of creating content. Ask yourself, "How does this content help further my business goals?" As Gregory does at CustomInk, define the goal of each particular piece of content. Some content may only be intended to capture leads. Other content's intent may be to convert a lead to a sale. One way to ensure that you have full content coverage for each goal at each stage of the buyer journey is to simply map the content you have against each persona and buyer journey phase or goal. Mapping the content can provide you with a 360-degree view of what content you have, its timeliness and relevancy, and how it maps to various audiences and their respective customer journeys. Figure 8.4 demonstrates a sample content map based by customer buying stage and persona demographics, such as industry and company size.

By organizing the content by persona data points, such as industry, company size, service, and buying cycle stage, we can easily identify content that still needs to be developed to address specific buyer issues throughout the process.

Also consider the content format when planning your content for your campaigns. The content format will also be important when choosing campaign channels, because certain content formats tend to perform best on certain content channels. For example, whitepapers outperform live webinars as a content format at driving conversions for Marketing Mojo on LinkedIn. You may need to test various formats over time to see which content formats resonate best with personas on different channels.

Certain content formats can also create unintended issues in your campaign. PDFs, for example, are indexable by default by most search engines, including Google. If you are using PDFs for lead generation purposes, ensure you are implementing the PDFs in a strategic manner. If PDF content is gated with a form and visitors are expected to complete the form to view the PDF content, then you likely don't want that PDF visible directly to the search engines.

In the case of one client, we found that over 35% of the client's organic traffic was being generated through direct clicks in Google on PDF organic search results. Figure 8.5 reveals that this client had over

Industry	Company Size	Related Service	Stage	Content Asset	Content Type	Publish
All	Small to large	SEO	Awareness	Mobile Usability Checklist: What to Do NOW to Optimize Your Website for Mobile Search	Checklist	4/14/2015
All	Small to large	SEO	Awareness	The Definitive Guide to Implementing Rich Snippets	Guide	9/9/2014
All	Small to large	SEO	Awareness	Ten Years of SEO	Infographics	12/16/2015
All	Small to large	SEO	Awareness	Is Your Website the Victim of a Google Panda or Penguin Algorithm Update?	Infographics	12/4/2014
All	Small to medium	SEO/Content Marketing	Awareness	How Search Engine Marketing and Content Marketing Work Together	Infographics	12/17/2013
All	Small	SEO	Awareness	Small Business SEO Guide		
All	Small	SEO	Awareness	Advanced Strategies for SEO		
Ecommerce	Small to large	SEO	Consideration	Holmes Products Increases Online Revenue from Organic Search by 28%	Case Studies	5/6/2016
Ecommerce	Small to large	SEO	Consideration	Oster Uses SEO to Increase Site Revenue by 93%	Case Studies	12/7/2016
Ecommerce	Small to large	SEO	Consideration	How FoodSaver Increased Organic Traffic & Revenue from Its Product Pages	Case Studies	3/15/2016
Ecommerce	Small to large	SEO	Consideration	Crock-Pot Increases Organic Search Traffic and Revenue	Case Studies	2/10/2016
All	Small to large	SEO	Consideration	Beacon Hill Increases Organic Traffic Through Page Speed Optimization	Case Studies	9/3/2015
All	Small to large	SEO	Consideration	How Video Increased Organic Traffic for Petrochem by Over 300%	Case Studies	3/3/2014
All	Small to large	SEO	Consideration	Marketing Mojo Restores Top Google Rankings for Mazda	Case Studies	2/6/2014
All	Small to large	SEO	Consideration	SEO Agency Checklist	Checklist	12/19/2013
All	Small to large	SEO	Decision	Marketing Mojo Service-focused document- collection of case studies for a SEO		
All	Small to large	SEO Audit	Decision	SEO Audit Offer		
All	Small to large	SEO	Loyalty/Advocate	How to Recover from the Google Mobile Ranking Update	Training Courses	

FIGURE 8.4 Sample Content Mapping Using a Spreadsheet.

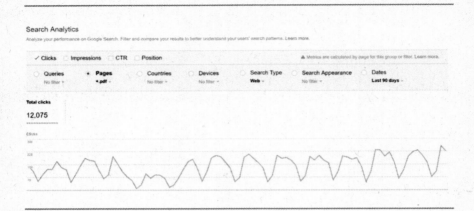

Search Analytics

Analyze your performance on Google Search. Filter and compare your results to better understand your users' search patterns. Learn more.

✓ Clicks	Impressions	CTR	Position				⚠ Metrics are calculated by page for this group or filter. Learn more.
Queries	• **Pages**	Countries	Devices	Search Type	Search Appearance	Dates
No filter ▾	**▸.pdf** ▾	No filter ▾	No filter ▾	**Web** ▾	No filter ▾	**Last 90 days** ▾

Total clicks

12,075

FIGURE 8.5   Google Search Console.

12,000 direct organic search clicks to its site over 90 days from PDFs ranked organically in Google. Most of the PDFs were gated with a lead generation form, yet searchers could bypass the lead generation form and access the content directly through Google organic search.

With over 12,000 clicks to this PDF content, which was mainly gated whitepapers, over a 90-day period, this client potentially lost thousands of potential leads as searchers were able to find the content directly without being required to fill out the lead generation form. That's a lot of missed opportunity for lead generation.

As we create content for the buyer journey, it's important to involve the sales team in the content plan. There will be content needs from the sales team as they continue to qualify and make the sale. According to the LinkedIn "State of Sales 2018" study, the sales team's priorities for content type skew toward websites and videos as forms of digital content to influence potential buyers.

Not all content is evergreen, though, so content marketing expert Arnie Kuenn recommends revisiting your content mapping once per year. In his experience, Kuenn found that even after creating a strategic content map matched to the buyer journey, marketers' commitment to the content strategy and map often began to languish over time:

They start to lose focus on all of the things that you do need to keep track of, and pretty soon all they remember is that they need to produce a lot of content. They start producing a lot of content and they lose sight of what the goal of each piece of content should be. That's when things start going awry – I've seen it over and over again.

Strategically mapping your content to your goals and the customer funnel and sticking to that development plan may seem cumbersome, but setting adrift will likely be far worse.

While some create loads of content with clearly mapping that content to the buyer journey, others are eager to cut content with reckless abandon. Over time, organizations can develop deep reserves of content, and it can seem overwhelming to review and value each piece. However, investing time in content review can prevent you from discarding valuable content.

One of our clients was redesigning its website, and the marketing director was eager to consolidate the site's expanding content. As the nonprofit's SEO team, we advised that much of the content could likely be consolidated without many negative organic search repercussions. One page on the site in particular, though, held great importance for SEO and conversions. The page was simply a "facts" page – full of information about childhood hunger in the United States. The page was referenced and linked to by countless news organizations and publications. It also ranked as the featured answer snippet at the top of the Google results page for over 45 related search terms and ranked in the top 10 search results for over 318 other keywords. Overall, the page was the most organic search trafficked page on the site and, most importantly, led to the most donation conversions for the nonprofit. Once the client was informed of the importance of this single page in its marketing efforts and the revenue outcomes it generated, they wisely chose to keep the page active. However, without looking at the page's value overall, both for SEO and revenue generation, they might have just as easily removed it and lost all of that value.

3. Choose Distribution and Communication Channels

Jonathan Perelman, a former vice president for agency development at Buzzfeed, said, "Content is king, but distribution is queen and she wears the pants." In other words, content is certainly important, but how you distribute that content is just as important. You can create the best content for your prospects, but if they can't find it, what good does it do?

When selecting campaign channels, here again the buyer personas based on actual data guide us in determining the right platforms to reach the right audience. Where do your buyers hang out? Which channels are the right ones to reach them? For example, when targeting business professionals, paid advertising on LinkedIn can be very effective at targeting specific audiences based on their professional demographics, such as title, years of experience, skills, company size, and more.

Channels also have different audience focus. Social channels such as LinkedIn and Facebook help marketers target audiences based on demographics and identity, while search engines mostly capitalize on audience's demands. Ideally, as marketers, you want to reach the right buyer personas when they have an intent to purchase, often meaning a multichannel approach to combine the identity and intent. For example, the overlap of intent provided by search engines and identity provided by social media platforms can offer the right target audience As Figure 8.6 shows, the sweet spot of marketing can be found where they overlap, helping us to target the right person at the time they are in the market.

Additionally, various channels and platforms have different delivery mechanisms for ads and content as well as different ways to measure success. As you select and set up your channels, ensure that you know how your campaigns will be measured and that the measurement is consistent. For example, while Google Ads had conversion tracking capability in its platform as far back as 2007, LinkedIn Ads only added conversion tracking capability to its platform in 2016. Prior

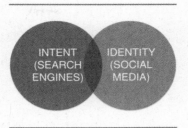

FIGURE 8.6 **Search engines show us someone's intent, and social media reveals someone's demographics and identity.**

to that time, LinkedIn advertisers had to determine alternative methods to the typical conversion tracking pixel that is frequently used by platforms to track actual conversions on the LinkedIn platform.

If a platform does not have conversion tracking capability, as was the case for LinkedIn ads prior to 2016, conversions can be tracked via a third-party tracking tool instead. Google Analytics (or other web analytics software) can be a viable alternative for tracking conversions across multiple platforms, especially if a platform does not offer its own conversion tracking capabilities. However, if you choose to track some platforms' conversions via web analytics and some platforms' conversions via the platform tracking pixel, it's vital to understand the method of the tracking to ensure you're tracking conversions consistently across the platforms.

We performed a digital advertising audit for a SaaS B2B software company utilizing Google Ads and Google Analytics. One of the benefits of Google Ads as a platform is that marketers can import their goals from Google Analytics and establish these goals as conversions for Google Ads tracking. This helps ensure consistency in goal tracking across the two platforms. However, this company had set up the Google Ads conversions separately from the Google Analytics goals.

When examining the tracking of the Google Ads conversions versus the Google Analytics goals, the most important goal for this company – the "schedule a demo" conversion action – was tracking inconsistently between the two platforms, because the URL of the

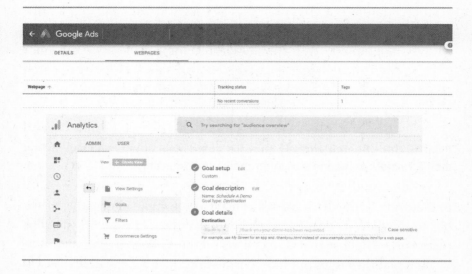

FIGURE 8.7   Different Tracking in Google Ads versus Google Analytics

destination page being tracked was inconsistent between the two platforms (see Figure 8.7).

This inconsistency leads not only to major reporting errors later in our analysis phase, but it also can lead to daily campaign mismanagement. As marketing team members manage the Google Ads account each day, ideally their aim is to optimize campaigns to achieve the most conversion, best conversion rate, and lowest cost per conversion. If the native platform conversion tracking is incorrect, this can provide a false positive effect and lead marketing staff to make misguided changes to budget allocation, providing financial fuel to less successful campaigns.

As the examples illustrate, data collection and data consistency forethought must be put into campaigns at setup as channels are chosen for the campaigns, and a plan needs to be in place to ensure that data is measured consistently across platforms.

As you collect data along the way, you may also find that you need to adjust channels. Many marketers place a heavy emphasis on paid search advertising. Yet search engines are often best at gauging a searcher's intent but are not always as successful at gauging identity. While search engines like Google tend to have more targeting options with demographics typically important for business-to-consumer (B2C) targeting, such as average income, gender, and age, the search engines often lack demographics associated with business-to-business (B2B) targeting. This can lead to high costs per click and per conversion because advertisers cannot target their buyer personas based on information such as someone's job title or company size, causing searchers of all backgrounds to click and convert on these ads, even if they are not the target buyer persona.

We saw this same issue for several of our B2B clients, including Julia's company at the time, ScienceLogic. The average cost per click on many of ScienceLogic's target keywords, such as "server monitoring software," cost as much as $24/click for Google Ads. We decided to expand to LinkedIn advertising to test if targeting business demographics through the social media channel would bring greater success. In the end, by utilizing each channel for its strength and shifting budgets accordingly, revenue increased 281% and sales pipeline increased 1178% even as cost per click dropped 83% and cost per lead dropped an astonishing 94% on LinkedIn.

EXECUTION PHASE

Once the development phase is complete, we're ready to move on to the execution phase and set our campaign in motion. Execution is where the rubber meets the road – where our plans are put into action. Plans and strategy are meaningless without purposeful execution of those plans.

1. Select, Prepare, and Optimize Your Tools

Confucius said, "The mechanic who would perfect his work must first sharpen his tools." Before you click the trigger and execute a campaign, make sure you've thought through the marketing strategy and then selected, prepared, and optimized your tools for the job.

Depending on the focus, distribution, and goals for the campaign, different software or marketing tools may be required to build and track data to measure outcomes. In other cases, you may need to acquire tools that can piece together information from various sources to get a full picture of your campaign's results.

To determine which tools are needed for the job, we have to start at the end. What are we trying to measure? Which tools are most effective to calculate those metrics?

As we mentioned when choosing channels, just as the channels we select have varying capabilities for targeting audiences and content formats, channels also have varying metrics they provide innate to the platform. This may require pulling in additional tools to either combine metrics from various platforms or to attain the desired metrics in an alternative tool to the platform itself.

Additionally, some of the data that you'll want to acquire from the campaign may not reside in the channel platforms or within tools owned by the marketing team. For example, sales data, such as opportunity and revenue data, are housed in the customer relationship management (CRM) system, such as Salesforce or Microsoft Dynamics. While the marketing team may have some access to the CRM system, these tools and their access are most often owned and controlled by the sales team.

What if your team is trying to plan an SEO effort? How do you decide on keywords? It would be helpful to know what keywords current customers use to find your company and convert. Unfortunately, Google and other search engines encrypt organic search results, so you can no longer ascertain through tools like Google Analytics which organic search keywords yielded conversions or even ecommerce purchases.

However, in this scenario, as well, there is a possible workaround to gain new learnings via other tools and channels. For example, if you have an existing paid search advertising campaign, you could start with seeing which keywords lead to conversions. But if you've planned ahead and planned out your tools, you could also ensure that your landing pages capture each converting prospect's paid search keyword in a hidden field on your lead generation forms and pass this data to your marketing automation system and/or your CRM tool, allowing you to run reports to see which keywords were most commonly used by customers who converted via paid search advertising. Knowing specifically which keywords actual customers used can help guide your SEO efforts through actual associated revenue data. But to gain these learnings means that you'll have to consider the tools you need early on and how they can enable you to glean useful information.

As your organization prepares campaigns for data collection, understand which tools are required along the customer journey measurement path and ensure that campaigns are set up to work with these tools, passing accurate information from the campaign to the measurement tool.

2. Collect Data Throughout the Campaign and Sales Process

In computer science, the term GIGO is an acronym for "Garbage In, Garbage Out," indicating that the data that you derive as output is only as reliable and accurate as the data that you input. In other words, if you put bad data into the computer, your output will also be flawed.

In marketing, accurate data output relies heavily on accurate data collection. With marketing highly intertwined with digital platforms, it seems that this would be a simple endeavor. However, precise data collection is often one of the most common errors marketers make. In turn, when the data input is incorrect, then the output data is also incorrect, causing marketers to realize false positives and make crucial budget and strategy decisions based on faulty output.

One of the more common tools that marketers use today for initial digital marketing data collection is Google Analytics, which provides marketers with a simple way to tag links from any campaign source to identify how traffic arrived at the website. Implemented incorrectly or overlooked entirely, Google Analytics tags (UTM tags) can provide marketers with erroneous or incomplete data.

In a digital ad audit for a customer, we found incorrect tagging had been applied. Figure 8.8 shows an example of a Google

	Source / Medium ⑦
☐	1. google / organic
☐	2. (direct) / (none)
☐	3. BingAds / cpc
☐	4. bing / organic
☐	5. google / cpc
☐	6. Capterra PPC / cpc
☐	7. LinkedIn / cpc
☐	8. AdWords / cpc
☐	9. m.facebook.com / referral
☐	10. facebook.com / referral

FIGURE 8.8 An Example of Tagging Applied Incorrectly for Google Analytics.

Analytics source/medium report. The sources of "google/cpc" and "AdWords/cpc" actually both represent traffic from Google Ads. However, the "google/cpc" source/medium was assigned in Google Ads through its auto-tagging process, which automatically appends Google Analytics tag data to each ad. Conversely the "AdWords/cpc" source medium was manually assigned to some ads by the client.

What problem does this cause? By splitting the total Google Ads traffic data between two tags, the client cannot rely on either tag for the aggregate data about traffic from this channel.

Source / Medium ?	Acquisition
	Users ? ↓
	8,116 % of Total: 1.47% (552,218)
1. LinkedIn / cpc	4,781 (58.58%)
2. linkedin / cpc	3,379 (41.40%)
3. linkedIn / cpc	1 (0.01%)

FIGURE 8.9   Additional Example of a Tagging Mistake in Google Analytics.

Tools also have certain idiosyncrasies with data collection that should be considered as well. For example, Google Analytics does not recognize capitalized text versus noncapitalized text as the same text. The source tag of "LinkedIn" and the source tag of "linkedin" will be identified as separate sources in Google Analytics (see Figure 8.9).

When planning and implementing tagging or other data collection techniques, it's also important to revisit our Data-First Marketing Campaign Framework and consider what measurements we'll need later in the flow. As the data-first marketing mantra advocates, ultimately our goal as marketers should be to contribute to the business' overall revenue goals. To truly know how campaigns are influencing revenue, however, we will need to track campaign data through to sale completion and revenue booking. For many marketers, this means tracking attribution beyond marketing's own tools through to the sales CRM. Only when a sale can be correctly attributed to one or many marketing campaigns will the marketing team know which campaigns were successful at influencing that revenue.

As mentioned in Chapter 5, establishing data policy is critical for marketing and sales to ensure that the data collected is accurate and usable. Before a lead even gets assigned to a salesperson, the marketing team's inbound marketing efforts must also adopt a data policy that is shared by the entire marketing team to safeguard against data inconsistencies.

3. Test and Experiment Throughout the Campaign

As we're collecting data throughout the campaign, we'll be able to see how the campaigns are performing over time. Not every campaign is going to be a winner out of the gate, and even those that appear to be performing well may still have further improvements that could increase performance. The only way to know is to test and experiment throughout the campaign.

It's important to note that "testing for testing's sake" is not encouraged. Rather, testing and experimentation should be approached similarly to how the scientific community tests. Scientists, on the whole, do not test without a goal in mind – a hypothesis. Each test or experiment follows a methodology that guides the test.

Tim Ash, author of two landing page optimization books and an early pioneer in the discipline of website conversion rate optimization (CRO), cautions that in a world where we're so focused on being data-driven, we can end up promoting and incentivizing the wrong behavior in our marketing organizations. Ash shared, "I had a client once describe CRO as a 'swim lane' – 'you have SEO, PPC, affiliate, and CRO.' But if you think of it as a tactical activity that's dashboard-based and measuring how many tests you crank out, you're totally missing the point." Testing for the sake of performing tests isn't going to help you win. Measuring testing velocity as a measurement simply isn't testing what matters. As Ash continues, "You really need to be testing to an economic threshold." Whatever tests you do choose to run need to demonstrate real ROI, otherwise, why are you doing them?

The goal, of course, is to continuously improve our campaigns to improve economic outcomes. As a discipline, science involves continuous improvement. The very definition of the word "science" includes the concept of experimentation and testing:

> The intellectual and practical activity encompassing the systematic study of the structure and behavior of the physical and natural world through observation and experiment.

As such, the scientific method was developed as a system not only for observation and experimentation but also to remove cognitive bias and assumptions that could taint the researcher from determining accurate and truthful outcomes. The scientific method is typically comprised of six basic steps:

1. Question
2. Hypothesis
3. Experimentation
4. Data Analysis
5. Conclusion
6. Repeat

Just as scientists may hold cognitive biases toward desired outcomes, marketers can possess cognitive bias and preference toward the outcomes they want to believe occurred based on a campaign execution. Therefore, much of the Data-First Marketing Campaign Framework mirrors the steps of the scientific method to help remove marketers' potential biases from the process.

A key component to the scientific method is the testing or experiment phase, and similarly in marketing, testing, and revision is necessary to refine the results. The Data-First Marketing Campaign Framework helps marketers achieve business goals through a process of continuous improvement. Businesses have long applied continuous improvement models to various parts of the organization. The popular Six Sigma uses continuous improvement to reduce inefficiencies that helps eliminate defects in products and process. Jack Welch made Six Sigma integral to business strategy at General Electric, reportedly saving the company over $12 billion in operational costs.

Other organizations found success with additional business models for continuous improvement. Toyota Corporation is renowned for its continuous improvement processes in manufacturing through "The Toyota Way," Toyota's managerial approach and production system. A key component of this system is *kaizen,* a Japanese word meaning "change for better," which has been applied to many areas, including business, to facilitate continual improvement. By applying the kaizen approach, Toyota realizes greater resource efficiency, and in the case of Toyota Saudi Arabia, Toyota saved $3.33 million by not having to invest in new facilities nor to increase the number of installers needed to meet the increase in demand.

Kaizen is modeled after the scientific method, a proven process consisting of systematic observation, measurement, and experimentation, and the formulation, testing, and modification of hypotheses. Kaizen and the foundations of the scientific method can also be specifically applied to marketing to encourage continuous improvement in the organization to reach our business marketing goals. Similarly, the Data-First Marketing Campaign Framework involves not only the execution of marketing tactics but also the continuous improvement of those tactics as measured against our business marketing strategy and business goals.

It's important to realize that there will be failures. But failure, and more importantly learning from failure, helps our marketing efforts improve, which is what the scientific method does for science. Not every hypothesis will be proven. Many will fail. It's uncommon that you might hit your goals on your first try. That's why we have testing and revision. As marketers, like scientists, we have to learn to embrace to prospect of failure to achieve improvement.

In his podcast, Success Through Failure, Jim Harshaw, Jr. examines the connections between failure and success in business and life through the lens of athletics. Harshaw was a former Division I All American wrestler and former Division I head coach at the University of Virginia and speaks around the country about the power of failure to drive success. Harshaw has interviewed many famous wrestlers, marketers, and business leaders for his podcast series. In business, as in athletics, Harshaw points out that continuous improvement in any field relies on seeking out failures:

> You work, day in and day out. Not for a day or a week but for as long as necessary to get the results you want. It's not easy. Nothing worth doing is.
>
> But you must seek failure.
>
> Failure teaches us where we need to improve.
>
> Failure is the common experience among anyone who's found success.
>
> Failure is the ingredient that any successful athlete, team, business leader, or organization must seek out as a tool for continuous improvement.

Expertise is as much about what *not* to do as what to do, and we gain expertise by trying, and failing, often.

Years ago, I (co-author Janet) was the director of digital marketing for an online survey company, WebSurveyor. Like many software-as-a-service companies, our business and marketing strategy goal was to convert more website visitors to free trials of our product. Free trials, we knew, led to purchases, resulting in revenue.

However, we had many preconceived notions about how site visitors wanted to interact with the site when they visited. Like many other websites of the day, our home page was strewn with multiple calls to action: news, events, case studies, user guides, and more (see Figure 8.10). It was easy for the main call to action – the free trial sign-up – to get lost in all of the other topics covered on the home page. Since the home page was the most trafficked page of our entire site, how could we convert more home page visitors to sign up for the free trial?

This is where A|B testing came in. A|B testing, or split testing, is a test with only two variants, A and B. A|B experiments test a hypothesis. In my test, I wanted to see if I could increase free trial sign-ups from home page visitors by making the design of the page simpler and easier to navigate.

At that time Microsoft had been running a marketing campaign with the tagline, "Where do you want to go today?" I found that concept fitting for the home page. In my estimation, the home page of a website is more akin to a table of contents – it takes you where you want to go. Typically, most of us don't intend to end our website journey on a home page; typically, we're seeking deeper information than a home page provides.

I decided to perform an A|B test on our home page using the mantra "Where do you want to go today?" (see 8.10 and 8.11. The idea was to make a second version of the home page that was far less complex than the current home page – to make the next step on the site visit clear and concise. The result was the following test home page (see Figure 8.11). Several days after I launched the new home page, our company's founder and CTO called me into his office. He

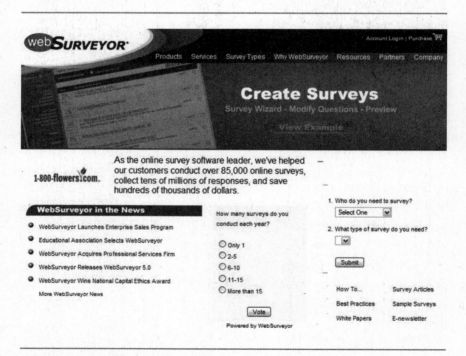

FIGURE 8.10   WebSurveyor's Original Home Page.

Source: Web Surveyor

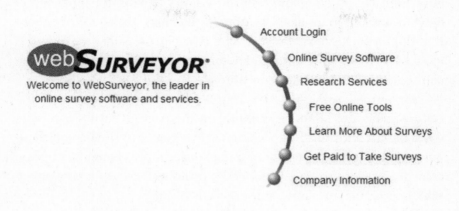

FIGURE 8.11   WebSurveyor's Test Home Page.

Source: Web Surveyor

clearly was not happy with the new home page design and told me to take it down immediately. I told him that I respected his feelings, but data from our A|B test was bearing out that the modified home page was outperforming the original home page at driving new free trial sign- ups by 50%.

In the end, the CTO agreed that the new home page should stay. But had I not tested my hypothesis – had I not had clear, accurate data to support my theory and argument – he would not have acquiesced. He, as many others did, held an internal bias that the traditional home page model was the best model. But that assumption did not hold true in the end, and testing allowed us to determine that.

Not all A|B tests require dramatic, sweeping changes such as testing two different website home pages. Some tests may be subtle but generate meaningful impact as well. Conversion rate optimization (CRO) is the systematic process of increasing the percentage of website visitors who respond to a particular call-to-action. In his book *The Big Red Fez: How to Make Any Web Site Better*, marketing guru Seth Godin compares website visitors looking for information on your website to monkeys looking for bananas. If the visitor cannot find the banana quickly on your site, that person will leave to find it elsewhere. CRO tests various elements to help make the banana (the call-to-action) easier to find on your site.

Sometimes something as simple as the mere color of the call-to-action can affect its visibility on the page. If a call-to-action's color blends with the page's colors, it won't necessarily be conspicuous on the page. In the case of one client, simply changing a button color from white to blue produced a profound effect on conversion rate, increasing newsletter subscriptions by 363%.

Remember our example earlier about content that was not performing? Figure 8.12 shows how content was generating organic search traffic but was not generating web bookings, which was the desired conversion action.

This represented an ideal opportunity to implement a CRO test to attempt to test new ways to encourage web bookings and help the content, which was already generating so many site visitors, to fulfill its mission and aid in converting those visitors to leads.

Regardless of what test you perform on your website, you'll need to start with the goal in mind. Like the scientific method forms a hypothesis about the outcome before the scientific experiment is performed, marketers must also know *what* they hope to achieve by performing the test. Ash also founded the strategic CRO agency SiteTuners. As he and his team approached testing and experimentation with clients, they asked three key questions: "What's the metric we're trying to optimize? And everyone has to sign off and agree. How will we measure success? And what does success look like?"

Beyond just performance changes, testing can also help the company make fundamental shifts that improve not just conversion rate but also increase revenue and lifetime value of customers. For example, perhaps testing a lower or higher price for a product yields increased sales. Ash shared, "You can optimize at the level of pricing, of the business model, of how much information you ask for and how you stage that ask." Here again, marketing's role in the organization

Landing Page	Acquisition			Behavior			Conversions Goal 1: Web Booking		
	Users	New Users	Sessions	Bounce Rate	Pages / Session	Avg. Session Duration	Web Booking (Goal 1 Conversion Rate)	Web Booking (Goal 1 Completions)	Web Booking (Goal 1 Value)
	292,854 % of Total: 10.66% (2,747,113)	283,387 % of Total: 10.37% (2,732,304)	317,664 % of Total: 8.85% (3,588,444)	88.45% Avg for View: 56.84% (55.62%)	1.23 Avg for View: 2.35 (-47.90%)	00:00:44 Avg for View: 00:02:07 (-65.66%)	0.02% Avg for View: 2.11% (-98.82%)	78 % of Total: 0.10% (75,704)	$0.00 % of Total: 0.00% ($0.00)
1.	18,134 (6.08%)	17,890 (6.31%)	18,910 (5.95%)	95.25%	1.06	00:00:19	0.00%	0 (0.00%)	$0.00 (0.00%)
2.	12,841 (4.30%)	12,504 (4.41%)	13,861 (4.36%)	95.13%	1.08	00:00:25	0.00%	0 (0.00%)	$0.00 (0.00%)
3.	12,274 (4.11%)	12,065 (4.26%)	12,891 (4.06%)	91.03%	1.16	00:00:29	0.00%	0 (0.00%)	$0.00 (0.00%)
4.	11,505 (3.86%)	11,369 (4.01%)	12,324 (3.88%)	80.66%	1.28	00:01:02	0.00%	0 (0.00%)	$0.00 (0.00%)
5.	9,825 (3.29%)	9,660 (3.41%)	10,600 (3.34%)	93.77%	1.10	00:00:26	0.00%	0 (0.00%)	$0.00 (0.00%)
6.	9,379 (3.14%)	9,013 (3.18%)	9,940 (3.13%)	94.87%	1.09	00:00:28	0.00%	0 (0.00%)	$0.00 (0.00%)
7.	8,884 (2.98%)	8,295 (2.93%)	9,581 (3.02%)	87.17%	1.21	00:00:49	0.00%	0 (0.00%)	$0.00 (0.00%)
8.	8,467 (2.84%)	8,388 (2.96%)	9,322 (2.93%)	89.29%	1.19	00:00:45	0.00%	0 (0.00%)	$0.00 (0.00%)
9.	8,367 (2.80%)	8,072 (2.85%)	8,712 (2.74%)	79.38%	1.53	00:01:21	0.00%	0 (0.00%)	$0.00 (0.00%)
10.	8,345 (2.80%)	7,713 (2.72%)	8,762 (2.76%)	87.71%	1.19	00:00:49	0.00%	0 (0.00%)	$0.00 (0.00%)

FIGURE 8.12   Organic Search Traffic Does Not Necessarily Generate Web Bookings.

and meeting its overall goals extends beyond just simply testing conversion rates; marketing can be a strategic partner to help the business learn and improve overall.

Ash shared a story of a client he worked with – a large RV rental company. They had a 17-page rental contract online – 17 screens long. He asked them to describe what happens in the rental process. The client proceeded to describe how the renter would fill out the contract online, and then when it came time to take possession of the RV for the rental period, the rental agent would walk around the RV with the renter to inspect it, train the renter on safety issues, and then print out and sign the final agreement. Ash realized that 80% of that process did not require the long contract before the rental occurred, because the rental agents were doing much in person anyway.

Ash proposed a fundamental business model change. Instead of the 17-page online contract, he recommended a shift to a reservation system that asks: how many people are going, where are you going to pick up the RV and drop it off, and where and when will you pick up the RV and drop it off? By making the change, they weren't actually changing what they sold, but it made the process easier and simpler for the customer.

In the end, the *right* testing performed in the *right* manner can help companies to improve not only marketing metric performance but ultimately improve business economic outcomes. Those changes may extend beyond marketing's traditional role of sales generation to even the most foundational elements of the business – the business model, processes, and pricing.

ANALYSIS PHASE

The analysis phase takes all that we've built in the campaign and begins to analyze measurements associated with campaign performance. Analysis, however, is not just regurgitating numbers from a platform, such as conversion rate, lead source, and so on. True analysis involves using metrics to simplify the complex – to identify what the data is telling you. There are three key focuses for the analysis phase: attribution, KPIs, and ROI.

1. Properly Attribute Leads and Sales for Accurate Analysis

Attribution focuses on how credit will be allotted for the campaigns and should be determined by the marketing team and adopted as a standard across all campaigns. Attribution should be ubiquitous – touching all aspects of campaigns and all types of campaigns.

But putting attribution into practice correctly can be incredibly difficult. First and foremost, correct attribution requires a common understanding between the marketing team and often other business stakeholders about which attribution model most closely represents actual outcomes for the business.

There are many various attribution models, but they all fall into one of three types: single-source, multi-source (also known as fractional attribution), and algorithmic. The type of attribution model used reflects the way in which the attribution model attributes credit to marketing sources. Single-source attribution models assign all of the marketing credit to a single source, typically the first marketing source that influenced a customer (first touch) or the last marketing source that influenced the customer (last touch). Multi-touch attribution models split the credit between multiple marketing sources, tracking each marketing source that influences a customer along the buyer journey. Algorithmic models use statistical modeling and machine learning to derive conversion probability.

According to the Ascend2 study "Measuring Marketing Attribution" from July 2018, while 81% of marketers realize that measuring marketing attribution is very important, many are still using very basic attribution models, which can lead to misleading data and analysis. More surprising, the Bizible 2018 State of Pipeline reported that nearly 44% of marketers still use a single-touch attribution method and over a quarter of marketers have no attribution model at all. That equates to over 72% of marketers who are not measuring the effectiveness of all of their content and campaigns along the buyer journey.

Using single-touch attribution methods is often a default for many organizations. Many campaign platforms and measurement tools encourage single-touch attribution through their standard settings. But single-touch attribution such as last-touch attribution

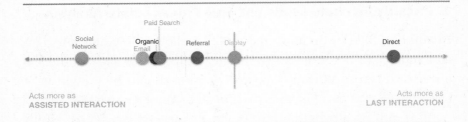

Paid Search, Social Network, Organic Email, Referral, Display, Direct, Acts more as ASSISTED INTERACTION, Acts more as LAST INTERACTION

FIGURE 8.13   Example of How Different Channels Are Often More Prevalent on One Side of the Attribution Spectrum Than the Other.

often gives too much credit to specific types of marketing content and channels, ignoring the contributions in the early funnel stages.

Google Analytics provides a helpful report that demonstrates the effectiveness of various marketing channel groupings by attribution model. We decided to examine marketing channels across all of our clients to see which marketing channels were more commonly represented in either last-touch or multi-touch attribution models (see Figure 8.13).

As our client data showed, many of the marketing channels acted more as an assist for initial lead conversion rather than the final lead conversion source. If we were to measure only through last-touch attribution, much of our marketing content and campaigns would look rather ineffective in this model, even though they did assist with conversion along the buyer journey. In the final assessment, single-touch attribution misses a large part of the marketing contribution to the buyer journey, leading to misleading metrics.

Regardless of the model chosen, it's critical to ensure that attribution is correctly being tracked throughout the buyer's journey. As a prospective buyer progresses through the steps of the journey and is touched by different campaigns along the way, the attribution for those touches must be recorded accurately to reflect the campaign influences on the journey. Correctly implemented, this approach provides marketers with a consistent and accurate understanding of campaign influence and a better measurement of campaign success.

In the case of one client, we were running a paid search campaign. Ad respondents were directed to the company's website, where they would fill out a form on the contact page, which filtered through the marketing automation system. While our team clearly saw conversions in the Google Ads platform where ad respondents had completed the contact form, the client reported absolutely no leads from Google Ads. Upon deeper investigation, we found that the contact form had a hidden field resetting the lead source to "website," which meant that all of our paid search visitors, as well as those from other marketing channels to that page, had their lead source overwritten by the form.

Other potential pitfalls for correctly tracking attribution may reside in your marketing automation system. Many marketing automation tools have "rule" features, allowing marketers to set rules not only for how to assign or treat an incoming lead but also what lead source and other fields should be assigned. For example, the marketing automation platform may assign the lead source "paid search" for any lead that uses a specific landing page that was designated as a landing page for paid search use.

In the case of a medical software client, the issue was not with a hidden field on the form but rather a rule set in the marketing automation system. Every lead coming through the website contact form page was attributed to "website" as opposed to its original, correct lead source based on a rule in the marketing automation system that assigned a lead source of "website" to all leads from that contact form.

Keep a close eye on these attribution mistakes. If you regularly pull your data from multiple sources and compare it, you should be able to spot most of the errors that may occur. However, it requires close review regularly to ensure your attribution data is tracking correctly. Incorrect attribution data will lead you to false positive and false negatives, and perhaps cause you to spend your marketing budget in channels or campaigns that are actually less successful than they seem.

Here again, as with many steps in the marketing campaign implementation, we may also need to rely on data from sources that are not owned by the marketing team. CRM data exhibiting lead qualification, opportunities, and revenue generation combined with accurate attribution tracking define for the marketing team not just which campaigns succeeded in generating leads but ultimately generated sales and revenue. Understanding the impact of our campaigns directly on revenue generation helps us as marketers to make more informed decisions to fund, adjust, or cancel campaigns as they relate to the ultimate goal of our business: revenue generation.

2. Determine KPIs and Analyze Campaign Success

The famous management consultant Peter Drucker said, "If it cannot be measured, it cannot be managed." Without a clear definition of the outcomes we seek, how can we analyze our data and know if our campaigns are successful?

Key performance indicators (KPIs) are quantifiable measurements that imply that a lead will become a sale and generate revenue. Every organization sets its own KPIs based on its own measure of a lead's behavioral value. For example, a KPI might be filling out a request for contact or a request for a demo. Those actions clearly would indicate a lead's interest in purchasing a product or service.

KPIs should be determined *prior* to the start of a campaign. As Tim Ash shared in similar instances regarding testing measurement, we also need to develop and gain acceptance of KPIs before our campaign even begins. However, eConsultancy reports 57% of marketers only sometimes or rarely determine KPIs before a campaign launch.

It's important to be judicious when determining your KPIs. Not every action that a visitor on your website takes is a key indicator, and sometimes actions that you assume should be KPIs are not good indicators at all. At our own company, for example, we thought that blog readers were more likely to become customers. For many years, blog readership was strong, and we invested significant time and resources into the blog.

But like all marketing efforts, content creation efforts, including blog post creation, is an investment of time, money, and human resources. Because our account managers authored the blog posts, each post also meant sacrificing some level of client attention from that account manager to dedicate time to writing a blog post. We decided to determine if our blog investment was worth this significant investment. Was the blog actually generating leads for our company?

We examined three-years' worth of data from Google Analytics. The question we wanted to answer: "Do visitors to the blog convert to become leads?" In other words, is blog interaction a key performance indicator that would signify that the visitor is likely to become a lead?

As the data shows in Figure 8.14, the blog experienced significant traffic during this timeframe. However, during those four years, not one blog visitor became a lead, as shown by the goal completions metric. The goal completions metric included any type of conversion on the site that required the visitor to provide personal data, including e-newsletter sign-ups and contact forms as well as more significant

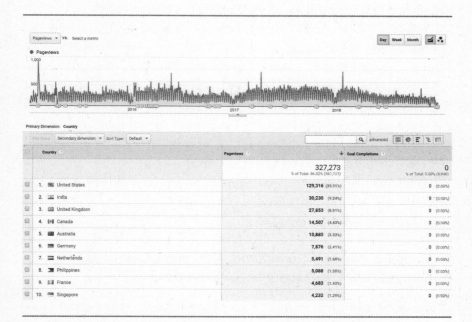

FIGURE 8.14   Traffic by Country to the Marketing Mojo Blog.

conversions such as a quote request. Additionally, while the majority of the blog traffic during that timeframe from any one country was from the United States, countries outside of the US actually made up the majority of the blog traffic. Given that our company did not sell internationally at that time, the blog content, while popular, was generating mostly traffic from visitors who were not likely to become customers.

In the end, the data showed us that, in fact, blog visits were *not* indicators of the likelihood of conversion. Understanding this data helps us further understand which website actions are truly KPIs and which are not. Furthermore, it helps us to determine where our resources – time, staff, and budget – should be spent, and, in the case of the blog, those resources are likely best utilized toward other marketing campaigns and initiatives.

Digital marketers also often rely on data points for KPIs that may or may not truly measure a campaign's impact. According to a LinkedIn study of B2B marketers, "The Long and Short of ROI," digital marketers tend to rely on click through rate (CTR) and cost per click (CPC) regardless of the campaign's objectives.

While CTR and CPC certainly help measure certain campaign outcomes, do these data points as KPIs accurately measure the campaign goal? For example, if generating leads is the goal of the campaign, why would CTR or CPC matter? CPC is a measure of the average cost to the advertiser for a click on its ad. CPC shows no outcome or connection to a lead being generated. Yet in the study, 42% of marketers of digital marketers with a lead generation objective claimed to use CPC as their ROI metric.

While ROI is our ultimate campaign outcome and goal, KPIs can provide valuable insight into campaign performance, if the correct metrics are utilized for analysis.

3. Measure Revenue Generation, ROI, and Lifetime Value to Analyze How Campaigns Impact the Business

While KPIs can give us indicators of possible revenue generation, they are only fuzzy indicators, not actual revenue generation metrics. Ultimately our analysis should measure if the campaigns are achieving the business and marketing strategy desired outcomes, meaning that we must also measure to the sales metrics and revenue generation.

Marketers are harnessed to the data available through the platforms and technology available to us. What you can analyze is also a product of the tools you have and the integration between that data. While the ultimate goal may be to analyze the return on investment (ROI) of each piece of content, each campaign, or each marketing platform, you may have to begin with initial conversion data.

However, marketers today also need to be sure that they're allowing enough time to accurately measure ROI outcomes. Because so many of our digital tools today default to monthly or 30-day increments for measurement, many digital marketers report in these increments as well. According to the 2019 LinkedIn study, digital marketers are often measuring ROI too quickly. According to the survey, the average sales cycle to acquire new customers for most B2B companies is six months or more, yet 77% of digital marketers are trying to measure ROI within the first months of a campaign.

Because the true ROI could not be measured in 30 days' time, digital marketers incorrectly conflated ROI with KPIs, which demonstrated at least short-term outcomes.

In some cases, you may find, unfortunately, that your campaigns are actually ROI negative – that they are not producing revenue. In the case of our client BookCircus, an online college textbook retailer, we found that paid search advertising wasn't producing the ROI we needed. The profit margins for college textbook sales are often razor-thin, and the increasing competition on paid search advertising was driving up bids and causing the campaigns to be ROI negative.

Situations like BookCircus can be very scary to marketers. Being accountable to ROI means you have to admit when something doesn't work. That's not necessarily a marketer's fault, but it is our responsibility to correct. Correction may mean alternative channels or testing a change in business model. But it is critical that we be honest and forthright about the data and how campaigns are ultimately helping the company.

ROI for one campaign, however, does not need to be our only measure. If a channel can generate high lifetime value, it is still valuable, even if one campaign didn't work out. At WebSurveyor we found that while Google generated a higher quantity of new leads, Bing generated a higher lifetime value. Marketers might initially discount Bing's performance based on initial numbers – it just didn't generate the quantity of leads or revenue that Google did. But Bing was actually more valuable for the longer term, because it generated higher lifetime value customers – those that purchased our platform repeatedly over many years. Understanding and digging deep into your campaign data can give you those insights.

Your measurement and analysis may be handcuffed by the data available to it. But as the Arthur Ashe quote encourages, "Start where you are. Use what you have. Do what you can." Start with the measurement platforms you have. Learn what you need to complete the analytic picture. Do what you can today but use the continuous improvement mantra to continue to improve the measurement output and thus your analytical view.

GET STARTED TODAY

To get started using the campaign framework, you can reexamine existing campaigns or start with new campaigns. Either way, start by defining that campaign's goals, which should somehow contribute to your overall business goals and objectives.

1. Determine the Campaign's Goal and How to Quantitatively Measure It

What is the goal of the campaign? At minimum, try to get a conversion of some sort. Even if you are only capturing an email address, that email can be used to further reach out to that person, through email marketing, contact targeting ads, and more. As Kuenn shares, "Every type of content should be generating a conversion of some type, even if it's a simple blog post. If you're going to take the time to create great content, the goal should be a conversion. A conversion could be that someone simply signs up for your blog. You create enough interest that they look for a way to engage with you."

What does success look like? Ensure you have accurate measurement methods in place to measure quantitatively the metrics that match your goal. If you're measuring conversions, for example, you may only need your analytics tool, but for more complex campaign goals, you may need additional tools and resources. Ensure that you've got the proper tracking in place to measure those platforms for correct attribution from the beginning.

2. Determine the Target Audience (Buyer Persona)

Know thy audience. What are their demographics and pain points? This information will help unveil the customer journey and the content and channels you'll need to reach that audience with the right messages at the right time.

3. Determine the Content to Match the Campaign and Customer Journey and Choose the Channels Appropriate for That Persona

Once you know your audience and their specific buying journey(s), map out each journey and the content needed at each stage of that journey. Choose the channels appropriate for that buyer and ensure that the content message reaches the prospect at the right time.

4. Measure, Evaluate, and Tweak

Measure the effects of your campaign. Take periodic measurements to monitor and evaluate campaign performance. Perform A|B tests to tweak campaigns to improve performance.

CHAPTER 9

Step 5: Data-First Marketing Staffing and Culture

Former Microsoft CEO Steve Ballmer said, "All companies of any size have to continue to push to make sure you get the right leaders, the right team, the right people to be fast acting, and fast moving in the marketplace." Nothing could be truer for the marketing organization as it shifts to a data-first marketing organization.

Achieving the shift to a revenue-centric marketing organization isn't going to happen overnight. This is a pervasive technological and cultural shift for the marketing department. It involves a whole new way of looking at planning and executing marketing. Most of all, it requires us as marketers to accept a level of accountability we may have been unwilling or afraid to accept in the past. By accepting that responsibility, however, we stand to gain the trust and confidence of our company leadership, sales, and the entire organization.

In this chapter, we'll examine how to build your data-first marketing team. It starts with marketing leadership promoting the data-first marketing strategy as the new standard. We'll share how to assess your current team – do you work with your current team members or find new team members with specific skillsets? We'll cover how to evaluate skills and how to train and coach various skills and then empower your team to take action on the data they analyze. Now let's start building your data-first marketing team!

STARTING AT THE TOP: CMO AND MARKETING LEADERSHIP

Any profound, cultural, and systemic change begins with an organization's leaders. Change requires direction and support from the top levels of marketing leadership. In "The Rise of the DD-CMO: How Data-Driven CMOs Are Maximizing Performance" in *Martech Today*, Jim Yu (2018) declares that leading this type of shift "means more than just referencing data points to substantiate strategic decisions, however. It means implementing rigorous processes, working with the right technology partners and maintaining a focus on genuine consumer problems that the business can solve."

To successfully lead the data-first marketing shift with the team requires support and endorsement from the highest levels of marketing leadership. In the article "10 Steps to Creating a Data-Driven Culture" in *Harvard Business Review*, David Waller (2020) proposes:

> Companies with strong data-driven cultures tend [to] have top managers who set an expectation that decisions must be anchored in data – that this is normal, not novel or exceptional. They lead through example.... These practices propagate downwards, as employees who want to be taken seriously have to communicate with senior leaders on their terms and in their language. The example set by a few at the top can catalyze substantial shifts in company-wide norms.

Marketing leadership sets the norms for the marketing team. Evangelizing and systemizing data-first marketing ensures adoption by the entire marketing team.

For the CMO, adopting and executing data-first marketing throughout the marketing organization holds the promise of something even greater: a seat at the strategic planning table. According to *Forbes,* marketing contributes 50% of all enterprise value, yet most CMOs are not involved today in the strategic direction and planning for the company.

But there's an opportunity to change that reality – to change the antiquated perceptions of marketing and its organizational value by espousing data-first marketing and providing the C-suite with the information that it needs to understand marketing's contribution and value. In a 2019 study by Deloitte, only 17% of C-suite executives reported having collaborated with CMOs over the year. The onus, however, falls on the CMO to reach out to colleagues in the C-suite to make connections, collaborate, and build that relationship.

CEOs can be a true ally in this relationship building effort. In a 2019 McKinsey and Company study, 83% of CEOs say that CMOs own the growth agenda. As Figure 9.1 shows, the Deloitte Insights C-Suite Survey found that out of all of the members of the C-suite, the CEO consistently has the highest opinion of the CMO. Make the case with measurable data with the CEO and enlist the CEO as your proponent to gain a seat at the corporate planning table.

The tools and technology can only take you so far. You'll need marketing staff that embraces data-first principles. As Apple's founder, Steve Jobs, said, "Technology is nothing. What's important is that you have a faith in people, that they're basically good and smart, and if you give them tools, they'll do wonderful things with them." Your team is only as strong as its players, but do you have the right players on your marketing team? Do they embrace analysis and continuous improvement?

First, you'll need to assess your existing team. Do you already have the right skillsets and mindsets in your current team to proceed with data-first marketing? Perhaps you have some team members that could be coached to achieve the necessary skills. Or do you need to hire new staff members to help you achieve your data-first marketing goals?

Assessing Your Existing Team

The Super Bowl is barely over each year before the NFL is beginning its focus on the next season. In late February, the league begins holding its official scouting events beginning with the NFL scouting

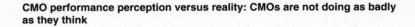

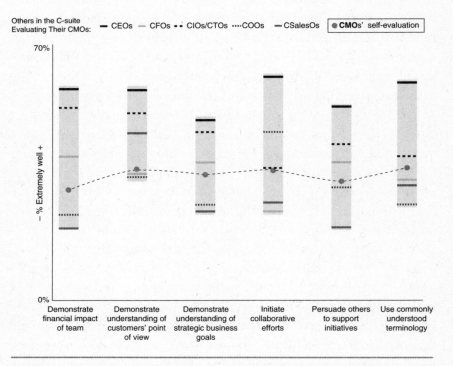

FIGURE 9.1   Above All Others in the C-Suite, CEOs Have the Highest Opinion of CMOs' Performance. Source: Deloitte.

combine. Prospective rookies from around the world converge and participate in a variety of skills challenges to demonstrate their abilities to team scouts and general managers. While scouts may have watched college players progress over the previous season, the combine gives the players a chance to showcase their abilities live.

The scouts and GMs then take their data back home to review in preparation for the NFL draft in April. The GMs, like in the Moneyball example with baseball, must assess what skills their team is lacking. What positions do they need to fill? A quarterback or a defensive end? What skillsets does the team need to succeed? Is the offensive line able to protect the quarterback? Armed with their needs and the data from the combine, GMs make decisions about which players to pick for the NFL draft.

When building our marketing team, we face the same challenge. Our teams, however, often encompass multiple types of members. Your marketing team may comprise in-house staff, freelancers, and agencies. As the marketing team shifts attention to focus on meeting business goals and accurately testing and measuring efforts, what roles need to change or need to be filled? Which players do we have? What are their skillsets? What is missing?

Assessing a team's skills can be especially difficult in digital marketing. When evaluating the team members and their skills, remember that most digital marketers are self-taught or learned their skills on the job. In "The State of Digital Marketing in Academia: An Examination of Marketing Curriculum's Response to Digital Disruption," Dr. Scott Cowley – a professor in the field of digital marketing and a former digital marketing practitioner – and his co-authors examined how digital marketing is being taught in US colleges and universities (Langan, Cowley, and Nguyen, 2019). Cowley's study reviewed all of the Association to Advance Collegiate Schools of Business (AACSB) accredited undergraduate business programs in the US. Of the 529 accredited business schools, the majority (56%) only offered one or two digital marketing classes and 27% offered no digital marketing classes at all. Additionally, only 6.3% of these schools require a marketing analytics course as part of the marketing degree.

This reality of digital marketing training for recent graduates creates a very real issue for marketing managers and leadership. While some employees may have developed strong digital and data skills over time through various experiences, the burden of training and coaching increasingly lies with the company and management versus traditional collegiate education.

Assessing Hard Skills and Soft Skills

Beyond the hard skills that are not always covered at the university level, being a data-first marketer requires soft skills, especially critical thinking skills. In a 2016 survey by Payscale, 60% of hiring managers listed critical thinking as the most commonly lacking soft skill among recent college graduates. A 2017 analysis by the *Wall Street Journal* further bolsters Payscale's findings. *WSJ* reviewed standardized test scores given to freshmen and seniors at 200 colleges and found that the average graduate from some of the most prestigious universities shows little or no improvement in critical thinking over four years.

As an employer myself who has hired hundreds of recent college graduates in my own agency, I (co-author Janet) agree with this conclusion. Unfortunately, most education today requires students to memorize and repeat facts, which doesn't address their problem: the lack of problem-solving and critical-thinking skills. Nevertheless, soft skills are much more difficult to teach compared to hard skills. Soft skills are teachable through a variety of methods, such as coaching, training, and leadership. However, there is a growing body of evidence that suggests that soft skills are a critical factor in determining people's training potential, learning potential, and coachability.

As you assess each team member for a data-first marketing transformation in your own organization, look for both hard and soft skills in the required skillset:

Hard Skills	**Soft Skills**
Knowledge and experience/expertise in: • Digital platforms • Excel • Using analytics platforms, like Google Analytics • HTML • Communication • Writing/Editing	• Curiosity • Critical thinking • Problem solving • Tenacity • Adaptability • Honesty/Integrity • Investigative mindset • Ability to ask for help • Growth mindset

Critical Thinking Roadmap

	BEGINNER	PROGRESSING	INTERMEDIATE	ADVANCED	THRESHOLD
EXECUTE	Understands and can re-articulate provided instructions	Completes assignments comprehensively (i.e., does everything asked of them)	Completes assignments at an acceptable quality level for someone of their tenure	Completes assignments on time	Makes suggestions for how to improve or add to their work
SYNTHESIZE	Identifies all the important insights	Excludes all unimportant insights	Accurately assesses the relative importance of the important insights	Communicates the important insights clearly and succinctly	Identifies implications of insights for future work
RECOMMEND	Always provides recommendation(s) when sharing updates or asking for input	Demonstrates appreciation for the potential downsides of their recommendations	Demonstrates consideration for several alternatives to their recommendations	Backs recommendations with strong, sensible reasoning	Makes reasonable recommendations on work that is not their own
GENERATE	Thinks up high-value work that doesn't follow logically from work they are already doing	Figures out to answer questions their supervisors have but don't know the answer to	Converts supervisors' and others' visions into feasible plans for realizing those visions	Generates own vision and communicates it in a compelling, easy to understand way	Helps others generate, clarify, and sharpen their own visions

FIGURE 9.2   Zarvana's Critical Thinking Roadmap.

Source: Zarvana.

Hard skills may be easier to evaluate; it can be pretty clear through testing and execution if an employee understands how to use a digital platform or Excel correctly. But how can you evaluate employees' soft skills? Zarvana Resources, a productivity app, training, and coaching service, has an invaluable roadmap to help you evaluate employees' critical thinking skills (see Figure 9.2).

After evaluating employees' hard and soft skills, you'll divide staff into three groups to categorize the marketing team members:

1. Has the required skills
2. Does not have the skills needed but could likely be trained/ coached to develop the skills
3. Does not have the skills needed and could not be trained

Category 1: Has the Required Skills   Those who already possess the required hard and soft skills are the very marketers you'll need to help you set the example and adjust the standard for the marketing organization. As you train this group in the data-first marketing approach, look to them to become your mentors and coaches for others that need more development. Understand each staff member's greatest strengths to maximize how you utilize them in the overall structure and rollout.

Category 2: Has Some Skills, but Needs Training or Coaching

As you assess your team, you will likely find you have some team members who are excellent at performing certain tasks but may not be data-first marketing ready immediately. In these cases, it's likely best to formulate a plan to train and coach these employees to prepare them for the data-first marketing approach. In particular, we've found that many team members may execute tasks well, demonstrating their proficiency with particular tools or platforms; however, about 90% lack the soft skills to tackle data-first marketing. Should you train and coach them, or should you start fresh with new team members?

In 2016 the Society of Human Resource Management (SHRM) found that on average hiring a new employee cost $4,129 and took 42 days. That's a significant investment, and that's just the cost before training costs. Time to productivity is another hidden cost of hiring new employees. In one survey, HR professionals reported that it could take as long as eight months before an employee reached full productivity. As managers, if we can evolve raw talent through training and coaching as opposed to finding new talent, it's cheaper and faster for our teams to succeed.

To improve either or both hard and soft skills, it's important to communicate an improvement plan with the employee and measure improvement. This plan doesn't necessarily have to be as intimidating as a performance improvement plan (PIP), which can often be viewed negatively by employees. If your organization gives regular performance reviews, those reviews should lay out clear goals for an employee to advance career development. In addition to distinctly stating these goals on the performance review, the goals should be bolstered with specific, documented training programs and supported by mentoring and coaching initiatives.

If an employee is lacking in hard skills, these can often be improved through training, coaching, and practice. For example, if an employee is making mistakes with Google Ads, Google offers comprehensive and free online training for certification. Consider having that employee complete (or retake) the Google Ads certification process and pass the certification exam. Follow that by pairing the employee with an experienced manager skilled in Google Ads to help coach that employee and act as a mentor as needed. Give the employee some Google Ads accounts to manage. Have the manager use the Socratic method with the employee to ensure that the employee understands the goals of the Google Ads campaigns and what steps to take to meet those goals. What targeting should be used? What should be the message of the ad copy be? What is the call to action?

We've found that most experienced employees are not lacking in hard skills but rather in soft skills. This occurs in part because of lack of soft skills training and preparation in college and a lack of good management after college. Good managers can identify soft skill strengths and weaknesses in employees and try to coach them to get the right results. But unlike hard skills, there may not always be clear direction on how to help employees develop better critical thinking skills. Returning to Zarvana Resources' guidelines, once you've identified where an employee falls on the critical skills roadmap, you can then develop meaningful exercises to progress that employee's critical thinking skills (see Figure 9.3).

Janet has often identified coaching opportunities in the moment. For example, she holds monthly strategy meetings with the team during which she asks the team to share two positive improvements for that client from the previous month and two challenges that they're having difficulty with. The positives allow the team to celebrate success and identify possible case studies for development. This also allowed the team to identify the value our agency had given that client in the past month. The real crux of the meetings,

Critical Thinking Development Exercises

	BEGINNER	PROGRESSING	INTERMEDIATE	ADVANCED	THRESHOLD
EXECUTE	Ask them to rearticulate each assignment you give them before they begin	Make them break the assignment into sub-tasks. Approve sub-tasks before they begin work	Show examples of quality work and walk them through how their work differs	Ask them to estimate a duration for each sub-task and add each sub-task to their calendar	Require them to think should be done next or what could be done better
SYNTHESIZE	Give them many opportunities to do low-risk synthesis work	Ask them to revisit and cut out 25-50% of syntheses/ summaries they have written	Have them do resource-constrained thought experiments (e.g., what if you could only share one insight, what if you only had 5 minutes)	During updates, ask them to share insights first and in a succinct manner; interrupt them if they don't do it	Have them wrap-up internal, low-stakes team meetings
RECOMMEND	Always ask them what they think before answering their questions	After they make the case for their recommendations, ask them to make the case against their recommendations	When making recommendations, require them to propose 2-3 recommendations in the order they would recommend them	Have them to convey the logic behind their recommendations visually (e.g., in the form of a logic model)	During team meeting, ask them what they think should be done about others' work and have them answer others' questions
GENERATE	Tell them to keep a list of ideas they have for the team, project, and/or organization and share it regularly	When you run into a roadblock in your work, delegate solving it to them	Share only your vision for a project and have them create a plan to turn the vision into a reality	Regularly ask them: Where do you want this department/ organization to be in 1 year, 3 years?	Have them mentor less experienced, emerging leaders

FIGURE 9.3   Zarvana's Critical Thinking Development Exercises.
Source: Zarvana.

however, is the challenges portion. As the team shares what they may be struggling with, as a senior marketer, Janet helps them formulate ideas that may help them find the root of the problem and possible workarounds or solutions to that issue.

We recently had a new graduate join our agency. During several strategy meetings for digital advertising clients, when he would state his positives from the previous month, he would often highlight that the client had an increase in ad impressions over the last month. While greater impressions do mean greater brand exposure for that client, did *we* create that value for the client? Or were the increased impressions merely a side effect from the client's increased budget that month?

Being a new college grad, he had never really been taught that impressions are highly driven by platform and campaign spend. He also didn't really realize yet the importance of value metrics for the client. What does the client *really* care about? Likely not impressions, but rather how we improve conversion rates and lower costs per conversion. Moments like this help both identify training and coaching opportunities and often simply coaching in the moment for both hard and soft skills.

Category 3: Does Not Have the Required Skills and Cannot Be Trained Don't let the data from SHRM about the costs and time to ramp up a new employee scare you, however, from making tough decisions about team members who fall into category 3 – those who do not have the skills needed and cannot be trained. Just like in *Moneyball*, there are times that we must cut team members that are no longer the right fit for our team's future. As Billy Beane tells apprentice Peter Brand, firing isn't personal; "It's part of the job."

In his book *Fire Someone Today*, Bob Pritchett (2006) shares a story of when he had to fire an employee, John. He had tried moving John to every possible department in the company, but John just couldn't seem to achieve in any position he'd held. Pritchett knew he had to fire John, but he worried about how John would survive. How would John pay his bills and support his family? In the end, after Pritchett made the gut-wrenching decision and fired John, he later found out that being fired actually inspired John to evaluate his life and pursue his dream of joining the ministry. Pritchett writes, "In my foolish desire to take responsibility for John, I had helped keep him from his true calling for as much as a year after it was clear to me that he was in the wrong place."

Terminating an employee is never easy. But if you know that the team member is not the right fit, it is far better for the marketing team and the employee to recognize this and make the necessary change.

Hiring the Right Team

When assembling a data-first marketing team, you may require a combination of in-house and agency resources. A 2019 report by

Spear Marketing Group evaluated the "marketing talent crunch." Two main findings of the survey of over 10,000 B2B marketers revealed the following:

1. It's more difficult to find the right people for our own job openings.
2. Companies are looking to us (and other service providers, including contractors and freelancers) as both interim and permanent alternatives to hiring full-time employees.

As Figure 9.4 shows, the survey respondents also indicated that the most difficult skill to hire for right now is marketing analytics.

Working with an agency can help an organization fill those skill gaps that the organization has difficulty hiring with in-house marketing talent. Consider adding an agency to your mix in particular areas where you need specific expertise to round out your team.

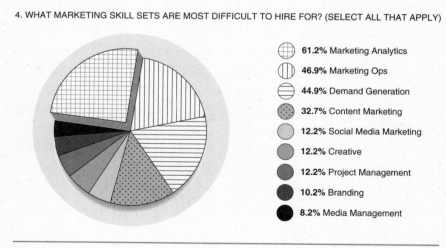

4. WHAT MARKETING SKILL SETS ARE MOST DIFFICULT TO HIRE FOR? (SELECT ALL THAT APPLY)

61.2% Marketing Analytics

46.9% Marketing Ops

44.9% Demand Generation

32.7% Content Marketing

12.2% Social Media Marketing

12.2% Creative

12.2% Project Management

10.2% Branding

8.2% Media Management

FIGURE 9.4   **Marketing Analytics Is the Most Difficult Position to Hire.**

Source: From Spear Marketing Group Report 2019.

Getting the Team Trained

Once you've assembled the right team, you'll need to train them in the data-first marketing approach, including the campaign framework described extensively in the previous chapter. This means helping the team reframe their current marketing approaches and embracing a new methodology and a new mindset. In his *HBR* article on creating a data-driven culture, David Waller proposed, "The biggest obstacles to creating data-based businesses aren't technical; they're cultural. It is simple enough to describe how to inject data into a decision-making process. It is far harder to make this normal, even automatic, for employees – a shift in mindset that presents a daunting challenge." How do you begin changing established marketing mindsets?

Getting the Right Mindset

Scientist Michael Faraday said, "There's nothing quite as frightening as someone who knows they are right." Even the most experienced among us continue to learn and develop over time. Just as growth and lifelong learning is essential for scientists to make new discoveries, it is also essential for marketers to continually improve their efforts over the course of their careers.

In 1988 Dr. Carol Dweck presented a research-based model on the impact that mindset has on pursuing and achieving performance goals. Dweck presented two base mindsets: fixed and growth. With the fixed mindset, individuals desire to appear intelligent but avoid challenges, ignore useful negative feedback, and feel threatened by others' success. As a result, those with a fixed mindset plateau early and achieve less than their full potential. Conversely, those with a growth mindset embrace challenges, persist in the face of setbacks, learn from criticisms, and find lessons and inspiration in the success of others. In the end, those with the growth mindset achieve a higher level of achievement.

When interviewing job candidates, one of the common questions we ask interviewees is "Why do you want to work here?" to understand what about our company appeals to them. Certainly, we often received canned answers, but we're looking for the person who genuinely shows interest in our company and what we do. In one interview with a college student interviewing for an entry-level position in search engine optimization at our company, I (co-author Janet) asked this standard question. His response was, "As an expert in search engine optimization, I want to bring my expertise to the company."

While this was likely a synthetic answer that would appeal to some companies, this student was interviewing for a position at a search engine optimization agency and was being interviewed by a search engine optimization expert with over twenty years of experience. We ended the interview there. This student, who had not yet even graduated with a bachelor's degree, already thought he was an expert on search engine optimization. His answer was all we needed to identify his mindset around search engine optimization – it was a fixed mindset.

Exhibiting qualities of one mindset or another may change from one activity to another. But it's critical as marketers to embrace a growth mindset to reach our full potential for ourselves and our teams to reach our goals. So how do we change our mindset in marketing? Multiple sources on changing mindsets suggest that one must be willing to accept new challenges. Using an established process such as the scientific method and internalizing it as a marketing organization can facilitate change.

If we revisit the Data-First Marketing Maturity Model (see Figure 9.5), you'll notice that the most mature data-first marketing teams have achieved a data-first mindset. They look for opportunities to test – to challenge their assumptions. And this mindset is *pervasive* through the marketing team.

Change begins at the top. How can you build an environment that fosters a marketing growth and data-first mindset and embraces established testing processes such as the scientific method? One key is to create an environment that accepts failure and learns from it. Remember that the growth mindset accepts challenges and learns from criticism and failures. Foster an environment that encourages this learning through your marketing leadership and how you encourage and teach your team.

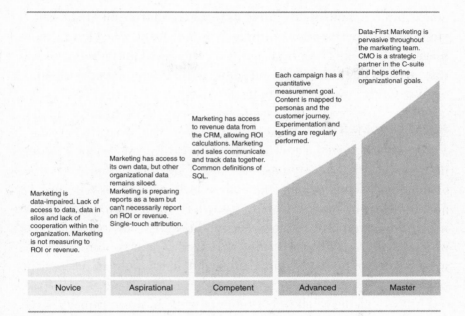

Data-First Marketing is pervasive throughout the marketing team. CMO is a strategic partner in the C-suite and helps define organizational goals.

Each campaign has a quantitative measurement goal. Content is mapped to personas and the customer journey. Experimentation and testing are regularly performed.

Marketing has access to revenue data from the CRM, allowing ROI calculations. Marketing and sales communicate and track data together. Common definitions of SQL.

Marketing has access to its own data, but other organizational data remains siloed. Marketing is preparing reports as a team but can't necessarily report on ROI or revenue. Single-touch attribution.

Marketing is data-impaired. Lack of access to data, data in silos and lack of cooperation within the organization. Marketing is not measuring to ROI or revenue.

| Novice | Aspirational | Competent | Advanced | Master |

FIGURE 9.5 **The Data-First Marketing Maturity Model.**

Consider the approach shared by Sara Blakely, the woman who created Spanx and became a billionaire. She credits some of her success to the one question her dad asked her every night. Some parents are content asking their children, "Did you have a good day?" or "What did you learn at school?" Not at the Blakely household. The question Sara and her brother had to answer night after night was this: "What did you fail at today?"

When there was no failure to report, Blakely's father would express disappointment. "What he did was redefine failure for my brother and me," Blakely told CNN's Anderson Cooper. "And instead of failure being the outcome, failure became not trying. And it forced me at a young age to want to push myself so much further out of my comfort zone."

The good news in all of this is that our brains actually have a system to subconsciously respond to micro-failures during task performance, and it directly links these micro-failures to improvement. In fact, a study of university students with high cumulative GPAs found a more pronounced link. Their brains sent off signals when failure is occurring, so they could regulate and improve their ongoing performance.

Hiring New Staff

For nearly ten years, Janet has guest-lectured and coached undergraduate marketing students in the Google Online Marketing Challenge. The challenge was an official competition hosted by Google that provided university students with hands-on experience using the Google Ads platform for actual clients. The students were provided up to $250 in Google Ads credits over a 21-day period to run campaigns for their clients and learn how to utilize the platform.

As part of the challenge, students wrote a pre-campaign strategy document and a post-campaign summary. The two documents, written before and after the 21-day marketing campaign, helped students project their goals and then assess if those goals were actually met. Inevitably, given that the students had little or no experience in setting digital marketing goals, many of the pre-campaign strategy documents had wildly high, unrealistic expectations. Undergraduates may not have even calculated ROI before, leading to grossly inflated revenue expectations.

In one report for a smoothie bar, the team stated that they would generate the following results through the campaigns:

Impressions	10,000
Average CTR	2.0%
Average CPC	$0.40
Budget	$250.00
Sales	$875.00
ROI	250%

The highest-priced item at the smoothie bar is $8.75. This means that the team is expecting to realize the following results (our extrapolated data in gray):

Impressions	10,000
Average CTR	2.0%
Clicks (Impressions x CTR)	200
Average CPC	$0.40
Budget	$250.00
Actual Spend (CPC x Clicks)	$80.00
Sales	$875.00
Assumed Quantity of Conversions – Minimum (Sales/Product Price)	100
Assumed Conversion Rate (Conversions/Clicks)	50.00%
Assumed Cost/Conversion (Actual Spend/Conv.)	$0.80
ROI	250%

While the students did calculate the ROI correctly, their revenue expectation of $875 was far too high for a three-week campaign and only a $250 budget at best. And how would they measure the actual revenue? How would they know that their campaigns are what generated the revenue?

This example illustrates why exercises like this are helpful to marketing students. Our agency came in, worked with the teams of students on their projects, and helped them realize the gaps in their logic and measurement by offering them our experience – experience they may not have gained in the classroom – to fully understand the goals that companies have with their digital advertising. In the ten years that we coached students in the challenge, James Madison University's teams earned the top global competition award twice and the Americas competition four times.

As we showed earlier in Cowley's research on business schools, it is rare that business schools offer even one digital marketing class.

Don't assume that staff you hire directly from an undergraduate or graduate program have learned the necessary data analysis to turn data into useful information. Like our experience with the Google challenge class, this group still needs further training and coaching to understand both the measurements that matter to the business and how to evaluate those measurements and goals realistically. They simply don't have the background or experience to know how to make these projections or to evaluate their meaning. That's why they need marketing leadership to further train and coach them to success in data-first marketing. Pair new employees with your established and successful managers and team members to give them the best chance at success.

When hiring new staff, experience truly is everything. But also, be wary that you cannot just trust that years of experience listed on a resume equate to knowledge and success. Before adding new marketing team members, take stock of their data measurement experience. Ask deep questions about this experience and how the candidate's efforts improved business outcomes. While you can certainly hire marketing team members based on past performance and perceived expertise, know that you still may need to coach and train experienced new hires in the data-first marketing process.

SYSTEMIZING DATA-FIRST MARKETING WITH THE MARKETING TEAM

Ensuring indoctrination in the data-first marketing process throughout the marketing organization requires systemic change. There are three main steps we've used to help teams adopt and embrace the data-first marketing approach.

1. Communicate and Train

First and foremost, it's critical that the marketing team understand the data-first marketing process and its goals. Share the Data-First Marketing Campaign Framework with your marketing team. Focus on how the framework specifically alters your current process. Discuss the importance of data-first marketing and what benefits it will bring to the organization and the marketing team.

Training isn't about just giving a slide presentation. Good employee training involves communication and education as well as practice and mastery. Some training may be available through third parties, such as certification training for various platforms. Other training, however, may require custom approaches in your organization.

2. Establish Documented Processes

To continue to entrench data-first marketing, you'll need to take the framework you covered in training and embed it into your marketing processes. This both bolsters the importance of the framework and allows team members to actively practice the framework daily. Using a project management tool, we've been able to customize and require certain tasks of each account team each month. The project task list is akin to a checklist of items to be completed for that client. Using this form of a documented process also reinforces the process over time.

Whether you use a project management tool to create a process checklist or you take an alternative approach, find ways to document the process and define responsibilities in that process by team member roles. For example, the content marketing team members may be responsible for the content stage of the campaign framework, but creating those content assets can't be performed in a vacuum for data-first marketing to work. The content marketers must also share tasks with the team's strategic planners and data analysts to ensure that their step in the campaign framework is successful in the overall campaign effort.

3. Integrate Expectations and Data into Employee Measurement

Incorporating certain measurements into employee reviews elevates those measurements to employee goals. Evaluating hard skills can generally be done using this method, with quantitative measurements. Additionally, however, it's important to set quantitative goals during the review and document these as well. For example, recent college graduates joining our Google Ads management team must attain Google Ads certification within a certain period. We set this goal, discuss it with the employee, and review the status of the goal during the next performance review.

But quantitative measurement of goals should also map to the mindset you want to create in your marketing organization. For example, to alter current mindsets around A|B testing and experimentation, consider adding this measurement to the employee review. Set specific goals, such as a goal number of A|B tests to run, to encourage the testing mindset.

Evaluating soft skills is typically more qualitative than quantitative. For these skills, you may want to solicit team feedback through a 360-degree feedback process. We've utilized a feedback form through survey software that allows various team members to provide a rubric rating for that team member for various soft skills, such as critical thinking. However, not all employees know how to give effective and useful feedback. To help fix this issue, we've held feedback training for employees using the book *Giving Effective Feedback* (*Harvard Business Review* 20-Minute Manager Series).

Management guru Peter Drucker once said, "If you can't measure it, you can't improve it." Whatever the method, incorporate the elements of the Data-First Marketing Campaign Framework into your employee development and measurement to emphasize its importance and assess their adoption and improvement.

EMPOWER YOUR MARKETING TEAM

The best leaders empower others. Once you've assembled and trained your team in the data-first marketing process, it's important to empower them to take action on their analysis.

In 2018 Forbes Insights released a study, "Data vs. Goliath," surveying business executives from global companies with revenues of over $1 billion per year. These are large, highly successful companies with capital to make the right investments. Fifty-four percent of the executives surveyed say their vision is one in which employees are rewarded for identifying and acting on opportunities identified through analytics. Further, 47% indicated that the ideal data-driven enterprise enables all employees to become data analysts, with less oversight required when making data-driven decisions.

Once the marketing team is trained in data-first marketing, processes are (re)established and team measurement is created, the marketing team is ready to tackle data-first marketing campaigns with less oversight. That doesn't mean, however, that marketing leaders can set up a team and assume that oversight should be completely annulled. Rather, management still needs to play a role in reviewing and approving data-driven decision-making. In part, this is again an opportunity for more seasoned managers to coach employees when they identify data errors or conflicts. The vast majority of executives in the Forbes Insights survey also only allowed action on data insights after consultation or approval by managers.

As you empower employees, consider adding review and consultation to your data-first processes along the way. Empowering employees does not equate to ignoring them and their work. Rather, active management, performed the right way, can empower staff as well as guide them to correct conclusions. In his book *It's Okay to Be the Boss*, author Bruce Tulgan suggests a method that we have employed in our own agency. Good employees begin with good managers, and Tulgan's approach recommends actively managing employees daily. We've adapted his approach, but staff still have brief daily meetings with their managers to ensure they are on track. We also employ the monthly strategy meetings, which allows Janet, as the agency leader, to hear from each employee and assess their grasp of the client's data. These strategy and manager sessions also provide an opportunity for senior staff to coach employees in the moment, guiding them to the correct data conclusions and actions.

Whatever management process you employ, be sure that you're actively managing your staff on a regular basis. It will help you continually assess their skills and allow you to help them improve before they take action.

GET STARTED TODAY

To shift your organization to a data-first marketing model, start with the following three steps.

1. Forge Relationships and Partnerships with the C-suite

To truly achieve data-first marketing, you'll need to know the organization's business goals. But beyond that, data-first marketing presents an opportunity for marketing and the CMO to emerge as growth leaders and key contributors to the overall strategy to meet the organization's goal. By integrating the C-suite into your strategy and planning and sharing with them metrics that matter to each colleague, you'll gain the trust, endorsement, and support of the organization.

2. Build Your Marketing Team

Assess your team. Are they the right team to implement data-first marketing? Where are the gaps? Evaluate the team and categorize members to know which team members can lead the data-first marketing initiatives and which need coaching and training. Hire new employees where there are clear skillset gaps, and consider a hybrid in-house and agency approach to ensure you always have the latest expertise as digital marketing rapidly evolves.

3. Institutionalize the Data-First Marketing Approach

Educate and inform the team about data-first marketing through communication and training. Reinforce and practice data-first marketing through process changes. Track progress and continue to emphasize the importance of the data-first marketing approach through employee goal setting and reviews.

Conclusion

Marketing is under tremendous pressure today, tasked with competing and winning in the digital marketplace and often unfairly judged for short-term failure. The CMOs' colleagues don't typically perceive marketing as a partner in developing the company's growth strategy. Organizations have begun replacing CMOs with chief growth officers (CGO), but just because the word "growth" is in a job title doesn't guarantee growth results.

As marketers, we've been touting "data-driven" marketing for a long time. Many of the concepts this book has put forth may seem like common sense. But if the concepts were so simple, why haven't marketers done it? Two main reasons: we're already busy and it's hard. If it were easy, everyone would be doing this already and doing it correctly. But now you've been given the specific framework to focus and execute data-first marketing campaigns, focusing you on the *right people*, the *right processes*, the *right technology*, the *right data*, and the *right mindset* to enable you to meet the business' goals.

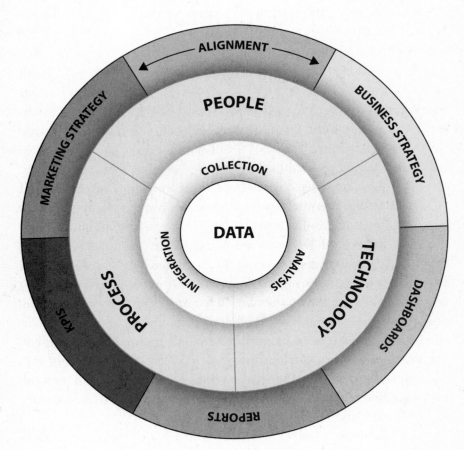

Data-First Marketing Framework.

By changing marketing's approach and applying data-first marketing to people, processes, technology, data, and mindset, you'll begin to change perceptions of marketing from cost center to revenue center. Marketers must begin to speak a common language with the C-suite and report on the metrics that are important to each executive. Remember that most C-suite executives are focused on *value* metrics as opposed to *volume* metrics. Your CFO doesn't care how many likes you have on Instagram; your CFO cares about revenue generation.

Speaking that common language also means that marketers can't assume that they have a good relationship with the sales team. All too often sales and marketing teams believe they are aligned, but revenue measurement shows that they are less aligned than they think. As with other members of the organization, involve the sales team in your marketing planning. Work closely with sales to develop a common definition of customer journey stages. Ensure that sales can provide access to key data you'll need to match business objectives and prove ROI and revenue generation.

Once you've defined the data you need, you'll need to evaluate if your current martech stack can provide you with the insight you need. Map out your stack and where the data you need can be found. What do you own? What holes are there that prevent you from measuring what you want and how you want it? As you collect data, be wary of your own possible biases, such as confirmation bias. Just because two sets of data may look like they are correlated doesn't mean that one definitively causes the other.

Given all the data we have to review and share with stakeholders, we must also be thoughtful of not only *which* data to share but also *how* we share that data. Our data needs to weave a compelling story for its audience. Consider how you visually present the data to ensure it is reviewed, absorbed, and accepted.

The people on your team are key to achieving data-first marketing transformation. As *Moneyball* showed us, having the right team doesn't have to mean investing large quantities of money. Rather focus on those with the right hard skills, soft skills, and mindsets to tackle the job. You'll need critical thinkers – people who regularly ask "why?" You may also need external experts, such as agencies, to help you build a hybrid team that can successfully execute data-first marketing principles. Once your team is in place, embed the data-first approach through training, coaching, processes, and employee measurement.

Follow the Data-First Marketing Campaign Framework. It's your team's guide to executing each element of campaigns, putting the *right* data at the forefront of your strategy, planning, and execution. Data-first marketing doesn't mean you have to abandon creativity and beauty; rather, it helps focus creative teams to channel their creativity toward a common goal. So be careful of putting form over function. A pretty website does not always equate to an effective website, as our Finish Line example demonstrates (see Chapter 7). Map your efforts to the sales and marketing funnel you co-define with sales. Creating a slew of content without mapping it to the customer journey is just a waste of time and money.

To recap, here's how you can get started today:

1. Understand and embrace the business' goals.
2. Rekindle the sales and marketing relationship.
3. Establish a reporting plan for key metrics.
4. Know what data you need to report on these key metrics.
5. Map and evaluate your current data sources to ensure you have access to the reporting data you need.
6. Determine where holes exist in your data access and address those issues.
7. Keep marketing metrics consistent from one reporting period to the next.
8. Experiment with graph/visualization styles.
9. Keep experimenting.
10. Always keep the end goal in sight – the business goals.
11. Determine each campaign's goal and how to quantitatively measure it before you start the campaign.
12. Determine the right target audience or buyer persona for the campaign.
13. Determine the content to match the campaign and customer journey and choose the channels appropriate for that persona.
14. Measure, evaluate, and tweak your campaign.
15. Forge relationships and partnerships with the C-suite.
16. Build your marketing team with a data-first marketing mindset.
17. Institutionalize the data-first marketing approach throughout the organization.

As playwright George Bernard Shaw said, "Progress is impossible without change, and those who cannot change their minds cannot change anything." Continuous improvement is as much a mindset as it is execution. Create an environment of testing. Test everything. Benchmark your team against itself. Continually strive for progress to reach the business' goals and ultimately ROI and revenue.

Even if you're a small company, you can do this. In fact, you may be more agile and able to move quickly. Think about the down and out Oakland A's, who had no real budget for the heavy hitters. They used data to their advantage and were able to compete with some of the most expensive rosters in Major League Baseball. And you can too with data-first marketing.

You're armed with what you need. We're rooting for you.

Now get out there and *win*.

Afterword

May 1, 2020

When we started to write this book, "data-driven" was a term that was still not widely used in marketing, although it was beginning to pick up more traction, and not just for large B2C companies. In the middle of the world crisis we find ourselves in now, "data-driven" is everywhere. Scientists, governors, newscasters, and more point to data to justify their actions, make their predictions, and explain the state of the world.

For all of us, this is a mixed crash course on the power of data – to both mislead and to illuminate. We saw a graph the other day that seemed to be showing explosive growth in the number of coronavirus cases in a state that, despite the data shown, was about to open up hair salons, tattoo parlors, and bowling alleys. It seemed like the news anchor used the graphic as an illustration of what he was saying, and we, as the viewers, were just supposed to believe it. It seemed to say, "I have a graph, so it must be true."

Here's what bothered us about that graph; it was labeled in a way that viewers couldn't see the actual numbers, so we did not know the scale being used. Is this exponential growth from 1 to 100 or 1 to 2,000? In this case, absolute numbers and not just the trend being shown would definitely make a difference in how viewers thought about this "data-driven" decision. And at the same time, the governor of that state kept saying that he was listening to the doctors and scientists and using data for his decisions. Could that be true? What data was he referring to? Clearly, he understood that he needed to justify his actions with data, but one thing we are all learning is that just referring to or showing data is not enough.

During this time, we also received an unsolicited sales email from an HR company with the subject line, "Costs – 52%; productivity + 73%; what more could you want?" Nowhere in the email did it actually explain where these numbers came from – perhaps a study or a case study, for instance. For this example of sales fail, it was enough just to throw out some numbers.

In marketing and in life, data is not useful on its own; it's the story that data can tell that is important. The danger for us all is when we start with the story and fit the data to match.

In order to be able to tell any credible story, you must be able to trust your data. Perhaps a better example of data used for public health is the smart thermometer, which, when paired with a phone app that shares data centrally, can generate real-time digital "heat maps" that can provide information on potential coronavirus outbreaks. Assuming the thermometer readings are accurate, this is data that over time can be compared against readings in the same area to show important trends that would give public officials and hospitals advance warning of surge demands.

In the end, we all need to be better consumers of data, and as marketers, better "keepers" of data. Tell the right story, surfaced by data, and that's how you'll get to data-driven decisions that make a difference.

Bibliography

Abdulmouti, Hassan. 2018. "Benefits of Kaizen to Business Excellence: Evidence from a Case Study." *Industrial Engineering & Management. March* 21, 2018.

Acunzo, Jay. 2018. *Break the Wheel: Question Best Practices, Hone Your Intuition, and Do Your Best Work*. Cambridge, MA: Unthinkable Media.

Allied Van Lines. 2013. "Allied HR IQ Announces Onboarding and Retention Results of 2013 Workforce Mobility Survey." http://www.prweb.com/releases/2013/10/prweb11260003.htm. October 23, 2013.

Allocadia. 2017. "Allocadia 2017 Marketing Performance Management Maturity Study." https://www.allocadia.com/wp-content/uploads/2019/04/All-MarketingMaturityReport-2019.pdf?x91899.

Altify. 2017. "The Business Performance Benchmark Study 2017". Altify website. https://cdn2.hubspot.net/hubfs/398755/Business%20Performance%20Benchmark%20Study%20-%20Executive%20Version.pdf.

Amazon. 2018. Formula 1 Case Study on amazon.com. https://aws.amazon.com/solutions/case-studies/formula-one/.

Ascend2. 2020. "Martech Stack Optimization: Strategies, Tactics & Trends." https://ascend2.com/wp-content/uploads/2020/01/Ascend2-MarTech-Stack-Optimization-Survey-Summary-Report-200122.pdf. February 2020.

Ascend2. 2018. "Measuring Marketing Attribution." https://ascend2.com/wp-content/uploads/2018/07/Ascend2-Measuring-Marketing-Attribution-Report-180702.pdf. July 2018.

Ascend2. 2018. "Account-Based Marketing Strategy." http://ascend2.com/wp-content/uploads/2018/01/Ascend2-Account-Based-Marketing-Strategy-Report-180108.pdf. January 2018.

Ascend2. 2017. "Content Marketing and Distribution." http://ascend2.com/wp-content/uploads/2017/06/Ascend2-Content-Marketing-and-Distribution-Report-170612.pdf. June 2017.

Barta, Thomas, and Barwise, Patrick. "Make Your Marketing Team a Revenue Center: 3 Tips." https://www.chiefmarketer.com/make-your-marketing-team-a-revenue-center-3-tips/. October 28, 2016.

Beal, Vangie. "single pane of glass" https://www.webopedia.com/TERM/S/single-pane-of-glass.html.

Belkin, Douglas. 2017. "Exclusive Test Data: Many Colleges Fail to Improve Critical-Thinking Skills." *Wall Street Journal. June* 5, 2017.

Bizible. 2018. "State of Pipeline Report | 2018." https://engage.marketo.com/rs/460-TDH-945/images/BZ-2018-State-of-Pipeline-Marketing-Report-Final.pdf

Blair, Adam. 2013. "Finish Line E-Commerce Hiccup Cost Retailer $3M in Lost Sales."
   Retail Info Systems. January 8, 2013.

Boudet, Julien, Cvetankovski, Biljana, Gregg, Brian, Heller, Jason, and Perrey, Jesko.
   2019. "Marketing's moment is now: The C-suite partnership to deliver on growth."
   https://www.mckinsey.com/business-functions/marketing-and-sales/our-insights/
   marketings-moment-is-now-the-c-suite-partnership-to-deliver-on-growth.   June
   2019.

Briggs, Simon. 2019. "Revealed: How data analytics is giving top players like Federer and
   Djokovic another edge on their rivals." *Telegraph. July* 1, 2019.

Bysani, Praveen. 2019. "Dealing with Cognitive biases: A data scientist perspective."
   Medium. June 23, 2019.

Chamorro-Premuzic, Tomas. 2018. "Can You Really Train Soft Skills? Some Answers
   From The Science Of Talent." https://www.forbes.com/sites/tomaspremuzic/2018/
   06/14/can-you-really-train-soft-skills-some-answers-from-the-science-of-talent/#
   35db26f5c460. June 14, 2018.

Cherry, Kendra. 2019. "Bandwagon Effect as a Cognitive Bias." *Verywell Mind. August*
   8, 2019.

CIO. 2020. "2020 State of the CIO Executive Summary." https://cdn2.hubspot.net/hubfs/
   1624046/2020%20State%20of%20the%20CIO%20Executive%20Summary™
   uscore;Final.pdf.

CIO. 2019. "CIOs Embrace Strategist Charter as Digital Business Matures." https://
   cdn2.hubspot.net/hubfs/1624046/State%20of%20the%20CIO2019_WP_final_
   online.pdf.

Dodd, David. 2018. "What Sales Needs from Marketing." https://www.business2commu
   nity.com/b2b-marketing/sales-needs-marketing-01993345. January 17, 2018.

Drucker, Peter. https://www.brainyquote.com/quotes/peter_drucker_154444.

Dweck, C. S.; Leggett, E. L. (1988). "A social-cognitive approach to motivation and per-
   sonality". *Psychological Review.* **95** (2): 256–273.

Edelstein, Stephen. 2019. "Formula One is adding cost caps in 2021, so teams are spending even more for 2020." *Digital Trends. November* 8, 2019.

Fernando, Dinesh. 2014. "Marks and Spencer's website redesign results in falling sales."
   Web Growth Consulting website. July 15, 2014. https://webgrowth.co.uk/marks-
   spencers-website-redesign-results-falling-sales/.

Forbes Insights and Treasure Data. 2018. "Data versus Goliath: Customer Data
   Strategies to Disrupt the Disruptors". Forbes website. http://forbesinfo.forbes
   .com/l/801473/2019-09-23/27jv/801473/8367/FI_Treasure_Data_Data_Versus_
   Goliath.pdf.

Gehring, William J., Goss, Brian, Coles, Michael G. H., Meyer, David E., and Donchin,
   Emanuel. 1993. "A Neural System for Error Detection and Compensation." *Psychological Science. November* 1, 1993.

Geier, Ben. 2015. "What Did We Learn from the Dotcom Stock Bubble of 2000?" *Time.
   March* 12, 2015.

Godin, Seth. 2002. *The Big Red Fez: How To Make Any Web Site Better.* New York: Free Press.

Haupert, Michael, and Winter, Kenneth. 2018. *"The Impact of the Blue Ribbon Panel on Collective Bargaining Agreements."* Article republished on SABR.org website. https://sabr.org/research/impact-blue-ribbon-panel-collective-bargaining-agreements.

Healy, Patrick. 2016. "Confirmation Bias: How It Affects Your Organization and How to Overcome It." *Harvard Business School Online. August* 18, 2016.

Hirsch, Jacob B. and Inzlicht, Michael. 2010. *Psychophysiology,* 47.

Iodine, Carlie. 2018. "Gartner Keynote: Do You Speak Data?" https://www.gartner.com/smarterwithgartner/gartner-keynote-do-you-speak-data/. March 5, 2018.

Ives, Nat. 2019. "Coca-Cola Resurrects Post of Chief Marketing Officer." *Wall Street Journal. December* 16, 2019.

Johnston, Keith. 2019. "Predictions 2020: CMOs Must Extend Their Span of Control in the Name of Customer Value." *Forrester blog. October* 28, 2019. https://go.forrester.com/blogs/predictions-2020-cmo-priorities/.

Korn Ferry. 2020. "Age and Tenure in the C-Suite: Korn Ferry Study Reveals Trends by Title and Industry." *Korn Ferry press release.* January 21, 2020. https://ir.kornferry.com/news-releases/news-release-details/age-and-tenure-c-suite-korn-ferry-study-reveals-trends-title-and.

LeadMD and Drift. 2019. "The LeadMD Sales and Marketing Alignment Survey: Benchmarking & Insights Report." https://www.leadmd.com/alignment/.

Langan, Ryan, Cowley, Scott, and Nguyen, Carlin. 2019. "The State of Digital Marketing in Academia: An Examination of Marketing Curriculum's Response to Digital Disruption." *Journal of Marketing Education. February* 17, 2019.

Lewis, Michael. 2003. *Moneyball: The Art of Winning an Unfair Game.* New York: W.W. Norton & Company.

LinkedIn. 2019. "The Long and Short of ROI: Why Measuring Quickly Poses Challenges for Digital Marketers." https://business.linkedin.com/content/dam/me/business/en-us/amp/marketing-solutions/images/marketing-roi/pdf/The_Long_and_Short_of_ROI.pdf. June 2019.

LinkedIn. 2018. "State of Sales 2018." https://business.linkedin.com/content/dam/me/business/en-us/sales-solutions/cx/2018/images/pdfs/state-of-sales-ebook.pdf.

McGarvey, John. 2014. "M&S shows the dangers of redesigning your website." *Tech-Donut. July* 14, 2014.

MGI, 2016. The Age of Analytics: Competing in a Data-Driven World. *McKinsey Global Institute/McKinskey & Co Executive Summary.* December 2016.

O'Donnell, J.T. "Here's Why These 3 Types of Workers Will Lose Their Jobs in the Next Recession." https://www.inc.com/jt-odonnell/heres-why-these-3-types-of-workers-will-lose-their-jobs-in-next-recession.html. October 4, 2017.

Ortiz-Ospina, Esteban. 2019. "The rise of social media." *Our World in Data. September* 18, 2019.

Pandey, Anshul Vikram; Manivannan, Anjali; Nov, Oded; Satterthwaite, Margaret; and Bertini, Enrico. 2014. "The Persuasive Power of Data Visualization." *IEEE Transactions on Visualization and Computer Graphics.* November 6, 2014.

Payscale. 2016. "2016 Workforce-Skills Preparedness Report." https://www.payscale .com/data-packages/job-skills. May 18, 2016.

Pemberton, Chris. 2018. "Key Findings from Gartner Marketing Analytics Survey 2018." *Gartner website. May* 16, 2018. https://www.gartner.com/en/marketing/ insights/articles/key-findings-from-gartner-marketing-analytics-survey-2018.

Pritchett, Bob. 2006. *Fire Someone Today: And Other Surprising Tactics for Making Your Business a Success.* Nashville, TN: Thomas Nelson, Inc.

Qaqish, Debbie. 2017. "3 Things Every CMO Needs For a Successful Relationship With the CFO." https://www.pedowitzgroup.com/3-things-every-cmo-needs-for-a-successful-relationship-with-the-cfo/. June 22, 2017.

Rankin, Jennifer. 2014. "Marks and Spencer sales hit by website woes ahead of shareholder AGM." *Guardian. July* 8, 2014.

Revella, Adele. 2015. *Buyer Personas: How to Gain Insight into Your Customer's Expectations, Align Your Marketing Strategies, and Win More Business.* Hoboken, NJ: John Wiley & Sons.

Sage Intacct. 2016. "Survey Reveals CFOs are Becoming More Strategic as They Manage Risk and Drive Business Sustainability." https://www.sageintacct.com/press/survey-reveals-cfos-are-becoming-more-strategic-they-manage-risk-and-drive-business. April 5, 2016.

Schouten, Cory. 2012. "Finish Line pulls plug on new website." *Indianapolis Business Journal. December* 20, 2012

Schultz, E. J. 2017. "Coke Global CMO to Depart Amid Leadership Changes." *AdAge. March* 23, 2017.

Scott, David Meerman. 2020. *The New Rules of Marketing and PR,* 7th ed. Hoboken, NJ: John Wiley& Sons.

Six Sigma. 2017. "Six Sigma Case Study: General Electric." https://www.6sigma.us/ge/ six-sigma-case-study-general-electric/. May 22, 2017.

Skinner, Ryan; Paderni, Luca; VanBoskirk, Shar; Overby, Christine Spivey; Merlivat, Samantha. 2013. "Put Distribution At The Heart Of Content Marketing." Forrester website. October 3, 2013. https://www.forrester.com/report/Put+Distribution+At+ The+Heart+Of+Content+Marketing/-/E-RES101981.

Society of Human Resource Management. 2016. "Average Cost-per-Hire for Companies Is $4,129, SHRM Survey Finds." https://www.shrm.org/about-shrm/press-room/ press-releases/pages/human-capital-benchmarking-report.aspx. August 3, 2016.

Sophisticated Marketer, *The.* 2019."The Secrets of Sales and Marketing Orchestration." https://www.flipsnack.com/SophisticatedMarketerQuarterly/the-sophisticated-marketer-quarterly-issue-5/full-view.html.

Spear Marketing Group. 2019. "2019 Marketing Talent Crunch Survey." http://info .spearmarketing.com/rs/902-DBM-891/images/SpearMarketing-2019-Marketing-Talent-Crunch-Survey-Report.pdf.

Starita, Laura. 2019. "4 Key Findings in the Annual Gartner CMO Spend Survey 2019-2020." *Gartner website. October* 3, 2019. https://www.gartner.com/en/marketing/insights/articles/4-key-findings-in-the-annual-gartner-cmo-spend-survey-2019-2020.

Steinberg, Leigh. 2015. "Changing the Game: The Rise of Sports Analytics." *Forbes. August* 18, 2015.

Televerde. 2017. "What Does Sales Need and Want from Marketing?." https://www.televerde.com/wp-content/uploads/2019/02/What-Does-Sales-Want-From-Marketing.pdf.

Tulgan, Bruce. 2007. *It's OK to Be The Boss: The Step-by-Step Guide to Becoming the Manager Your Employees Need.* New York: Collins.

Veenstra, Jennifer; O'Brien, Diana; and Murphy, Timothy. 2019. "The confident CMO: 3 ways to increase C-suite impact." https://www2.deloitte.com/us/en/pages/chief-marketing-officer/articles/confident-cmo-c-level-communication-impact.html?nc=1. September 19, 2019.

Waller, David. 2020. "10 Steps to Creating a Data-Driven Culture." https://hbr.org/2020/02/10-steps-to-creating-a-data-driven-culture. February 6, 2020.

Wikipedia. https://en.wikipedia.org/wiki/Chief_executive_officer.

Yu, Jim. 2018. "The rise of the DD-CMO: How data-driven CMOs are maximizing performance." https://martechtoday.com/the-rise-of-the-dd-cmo-how-data-driven-cmos-are-maximizing-performance-218693. July 24, 2018.

Acknowledgments

FROM JANET

Writing a book has always been a goal of mine, and I've been working on this book's concepts for the better part of fifteen years. Along the way, many people have helped shaped what this book became.

First and foremost were my parents. I was fortunate to have one of the first personal computers on the market because my father worked for Sperry Univac. Having this device in our home helped cultivate a love of technology in me. I want to thank my parents for giving me that gift and always encouraging me to learn and do more. They have always been my biggest supporters and fans.

I also would not have been able to write this book if I hadn't developed the confidence in myself over my youth and adult years. As a girl, I was a member of the Girl Scouts. The organization instilled the confidence in me that I truly believe has been foundational for me as an adult. I'm thankful for all that this organization gave me then, and still gives me today as a leader, trainer, and lifetime member. It excites me that now this great organization also teaches girls about technology and data – and that this next generation of young women will have that foundation as they enter adulthood and their chosen professions.

Another person I need to thank for helping grow my confidence is my friend and mentor, Tom Lueker. Tom has taught me much as a marketer, programmer, and entrepreneur, and I'm thankful for his friendship. It was one pivotal conversation I had with Tom that sparked a fire in me. When he was CMO at WebSurveyor, I approached him about attending a search engine conference. I was eager to learn from others. Tom told me, "You should be speaking at this conference – not just attending it. What makes the people on this panel more of an expert than you?" I have never forgotten that conversation. It led me to start my own digital marketing agency and to become a speaker at those conferences, and it led to this book. Thank you, Tom, for helping me see what I truly have to offer the world.

I want to also thank the many people who took a chance on me – the people who believed in me and have continued to be friends and supporters over the years. To Brett Tabke, the founder of Pubcon, for giving me my first speaking opportunity and for supporting me ever since. To Danny Sullivan, who also gave me so many speaking opportunities and the chance to write for *Search Engine Land*. To my friends at MarketingProfs, who have been a supportive group and platform to share my expertise over the years – thank you.

As I began to write this book, I reached out to many friends, who themselves have published books, to seek advice and counsel. Thank you to Ann Handley, who has been a friend and supporter over so many years, for her insights as I started down this path. To Andy Beal, thank you for many years of friendship and for your guidance on the book and publishing process. Thank you to Tim Ash, who was generous with his time, advice, and expertise during this process. I value your friendships so much, Ann, Andy, and Tim.

To all of the wonderful experts I interviewed for this book, you each added so much value to this book by sharing your expertise. I appreciate you each so much: Adele Revella, Arnie Kuenn, Jim Harshaw, and Jeff Gregory.

To my many collaborators, clients, and colleagues over the years – each of you taught me new lessons and helped me innovate and improve. Thank you.

Finally, writing a book is no simple task. It's a huge endeavor, and the journey is marked with stressful times. Thank you to my co-author, Julia, for working so diligently with me to bring our vision to reality. I genuinely appreciated your recommendations and guidance. I also want to thank all of my friends and family for supporting me throughout this journey – for encouraging me and keeping me going. Specifically, I want to thank my best friend, Patricia Delk-Mercer, who has been with me every step of the way and has been my constant cheerleader.

FROM JULIA

I'm a published author!

Just had to get that out in print. Writing a book is a monumental task. Well, I should clarify – starting a book is easy. I've probably started a dozen books over the years, since I first thought, "I should write a book." It's everything that happens after and then actually finishing which is the kicker. There's always one more thought you want to add, one more story you want to tell, so for keeping us on track, I thank our kind and knowledgeable team at Wiley – Brian, Chrissy, Vicki, and all the production people. If finishing a book and getting it published is a big feat in the best of times, you can only imagine what it has been like during the COVID-19 pandemic. Janet and I had debated the pros and cons of self-publishing and other types of publishers, but, in the end, Wiley was our first choice, and I am so grateful to have had their guidance for my first book!

To the many friends over the years who told me I should write a book: I did listen. For almost all of you, this isn't the book you were thinking I would write, but I still appreciate each and every one of you for always believing I could do it and telling me repeatedly I should. Now on to the books you think I should write.

To Natalie Robb – even before this book was a glimmer in our eyes, I had many wonderful discussions with this great data scientist who has the experience of a seasoned marketer. Her utter belief in the power and importance of marketing data analytics firmed up my own, and I thank her for contributing to the mindset that started this book.

To my co-author – Janet and I have known each other for many years, and we've "grown up" through much of this digital transformation together. I find it utterly satisfying that, together, we were able to write a book that distills so much of our hard-earned knowledge. She has my utmost respect for running her own business, and even more than that, for truly caring that every single employee has a path to advancement. For the time and the freedom to write and research (so much research) for this book, I thank you, Janet. I couldn't have done it without you.

And finally, to all of my friends who were my sounding board through this process – I am quite certain you had moments you wanted to roll your eyes at one more data or marketing story for which you had no frame of reference but made it through smiling because all you wanted to do was be supportive. I love you, and I thank you.

About the Authors

Janet Driscoll Miller is a renowned, award-winning speaker and writer on digital marketing. She has nearly 25 years of digital marketing experience and founded the digital marketing agency Marketing Mojo in 2005. She has worked with many top-tier clients, including National Geographic, Mazda USA, LexisNexis, and Activision. She is a regular guest lecturer at the University of Virginia and James Madison University, her alma mater. She previously authored a book on Google Analytics, *Getting Started with Google Analytics: How to Set Up Google Analytics Correctly from the Beginning*.

Outside of digital marketing, Janet is passionate about women's rights and building the next generation of female leaders. She is an active supporter of the Girl Scouts, serving as a troop leader, camp volunteer, and trainer. Janet resides just outside of Charlottesville, Virginia, with her husband, Tad; their two daughters, Emma and Molly; and their furry daughter, Daisy Mae.

Julia Lim is the vice president of marketing for Marketing Mojo, an award-winning digital marketing agency. Prior to that, she held executive positions in marketing and product marketing at several high-growth technology companies. As an early adopter of various digital marketing tools and tactics – from CRMs to marketing platforms to social media digital advertising – she has extensive hands-on experience with building martech infrastructures that support sales, achieve business goals, and display KPIs in meaningful ways for boards and the C-suite. She has an Honors AB degree from Harvard-Radcliffe and a MBA from MIT Sloan. Julia lives in Northern Virginia and has spoken about digital marketing, martech stacks, and sales-marketing alignment at local marketing events. *Data-First Marketing* is her debut book.

Index

Page references followed by *fig* indicate an illustration.

222   INDEX

McKinsey and Company (*continued*)
  McKinsey and Company study (2019), 71, 85
Measurements/metrics
  click through rates (CTRs), 168
  conversion rate optimization (CRO), 154, 159–160
  cost per clicks (CPCs), 38–39, 121*fig*, 149, 168
  C-suite focused on value vs. volume, 196
  Data-First Marketing Campaign Framework incorporated into employee, 192
  determine campaign goal and quantitative, 170–171
  digital marketing enabling precise, 15–16
  disconnect problem in different platforms for, 147–148*fig*
  email open rate, 38–39
  Google Analytics into Google Sheets swapping dimensions and, 104
  integrate data-first expectations into employee, 191–192
  key performance indicators (KPIs), 75*fig*, 76–79*fig*, 88, 166–168
  lifetime value, 94, 97, 160, 168–170
  LinkedIn's "The Long and Short of ROI" study on marketer use of, 168
  marketing, 44–45, 131, 161–162, 198
  pay-per-click calculations for digital advertising, 15
  periodic measure of your campaign, 171
  proper attribution for accurate analysis of, 163–166
  sabermetrics used by MLB teams, 31
  sales and marketing leads, 79–84
  value, 10–12, 44, 94, 97, 161, 168, 169, 182–183, 196
  vanity, 15, 30
  volume, 10–12, 44, 196
  website, 140, 163–166
  website traffic, 10–11, 38, 39, 120, 140

  See also Customer relationship management (CRM) tools; ROI (return on investment); Tracking
"Measuring Marketing Attribution" study (2018) [Ascend2], 163
MGI, 26, 27
Micro-failures, 187–188
Microsoft
  Microsoft Excel, 15, 101, 102*fig*
  Microsoft Power BI, 103
  ScienceLogic competition with, 35
Microsoft Excel
  conditionally formatted heat map in, 101, 102*fig*
  moving beyond spreadsheets of, 15
Mindsets
  continuous improvement, 199
  developing data-first, 185–188
  fixed vs. growth, 185, 186
  redefining micro-failures, 187–188
  successful campaigns require the right, 195
MIT Sports Analytics Conference (2019), 29
MLB (Major League Baseball) teams
  Florida Marlins, 110–112
  lessons for data-first marketing from, 31–39
  Moneyball: The Art of Winning an Unfair Game (Lewis) on, 31–33, 36, 110–112, 183, 197
  Oakland Athletics (A's) ability to compete with other, 31–33, 36, 37–39, 199
  using sabermetrics, 31
Moneyball: The Art of Winning an Unfair Game (Lewis), 31–33, 36, 110–112, 183, 197
Moneyball data-first marketing lessons
  1. defy convention, using data, 33–36
  2. becoming a contender using, 36
  3. always ask "Why?," 37–39
Multi-touch attribution models, 163, 164*fig*
MySpace, 22

ROI (return on investment) (*continued*)
 student challenge writing
  pre-campaign/post-campaign
  summary on, 188–190
 when reports are barrier to data-driven
  marketing, 45
 See also Business outcomes;
  Measurements/metrics

S

Sabermetrics, 31
Sales Accepted Leads (SALs)
 conversion rate and percentage
  changes, 126–129*fig*
 data analytics of, 123–129*fig*
 lead qualification funnel role of, 76*fig*
Sales data
 CRM (customer relationship
  management), 14, 79–84, 105–106,
  122
 how marketers rate their company's,
  83*fig*
 properly attribute for accurate analysis,
  163–166
Salesforce
 adapting and modifying, 105
 as major B2B sales CRM, 14
 sales and marketing measurements by,
  79–84
 Tableau, 22–24, 42, 103
Sales Generated Leads (SGLs), 78*fig*
Sales leadership
 assessing the CEO relationship with,
  60–61
 business–marketing alignment role of,
  71–73
Sales opportunities
 generated from campaign
  formula, 99
 opportunity volume KPI, 78*fig*
Sales Qualified Leads (SQLs)
 alignment between sales and
  marketing, 63–64
 assessing clear definition of, 53
 assessing sales team agreement of
  definition, 53

conversion rate and percentage
 changes, 126–129*fig*
data analysis of, 123–129*fig*
lead qualification funnel role of, 76*fig*
Sales teams
 assessing agreement of SQL definition,
  53
 business–marketing alignment role of,
  71–73
 guiding them toward data-first culture,
  48, 173–194
 marketers jointly planning with, 75*fig*
 sales benefits of combined efforts of
  marketing and, 137
 sharing sales and marketing
  measurements with marketing,
  79–84
 SQL alignment between marketing
  and, 63–64
 three main steps toward alignment
  with marketing, 87–88
 See also Employees; Marketing teams
Schouten, Cory, 115
ScienceLogic, 35, 36, 84, 112, 149
Scientific method, 155
Scott, David Meerman, 25
SEO (search engine optimization), 9–10,
 34, 35, 87, 138, 145
Shaw, George Bernard, 198–199
"Single pane of glass" decision-making, 99
Single-source attribution models,
 163–164*fig*
SiteTuners, 160
Six Signma, 156
Snapchat, 26
Social media
 customer data generated by, 20–21
 digital marketing generating new
  channels, 22
Society of Human Resource Management
 (SHRM), 180, 183
Soft skills
 assessing staff, 178–183
 critical thinking skills, 178, 179*fig*,
  182*fig*
 getting the right mindset to apply,
  185–188